TO

FROM

DATE

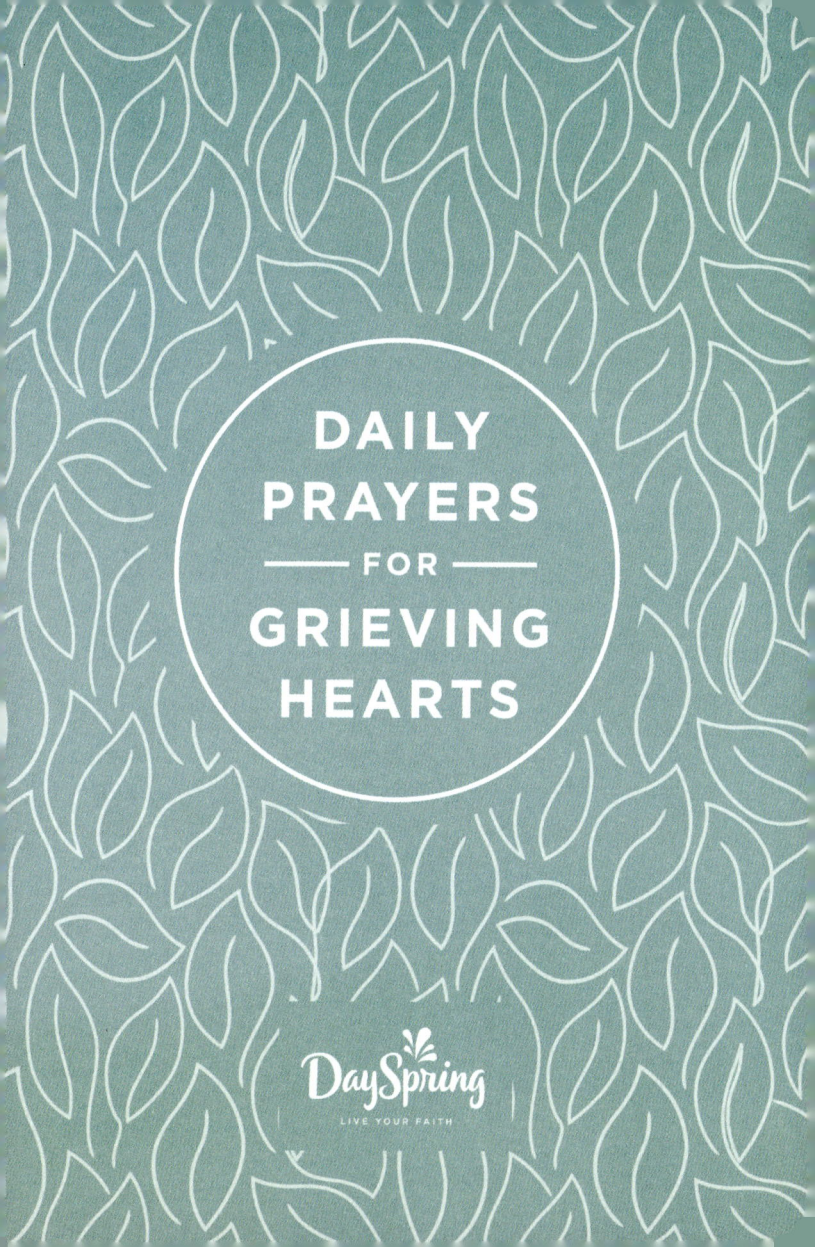

DAILY
PRAYERS
— FOR —
GRIEVING
HEARTS

DaySpring

LIVE YOUR FAITH

Daily Prayers for Grieving Hearts
Copyright © 2022 by DaySpring
First Edition, November 2022

Published by:

21154 Highway 16 East
Siloam Springs, AR 72761
dayspring.com

Written by: Lisa Stilwell
Cover Design by: Hannah Bedell

Printed in China
Prime: J9333
ISBN: 978-1-64870-844-2

CONTENTS

INTRODUCTION

One of the deepest complexities of life we all must face at some time or another is the tender condition of a grieving heart. Everyone is unique in how he or she responds to tragedy, and the road to recovery can range from loud and messy to bitter and isolating. The road to healing can last a few months or be a years-long journey—grief has no formula or cut-off date to count on or look forward to. In any case, living in grief can be arduous and cause one to wonder, *Where are You, God?*

Of course, His answer is, "I am here." Psalm 34:18 says that God is near the brokenhearted—He does not leave us alone to wallow through our pain.

He is an ever-present help in times of trouble, and if you are reading this, chances are you're struggling with grief yourself. More than anything, it's important to know that He is with you now, and He truly cares.

It is our prayer at DaySpring that, no matter your source of grief, you will find help and comfort in the pages ahead that lead even to the smallest deposit of the Savior's touch. May each reading be a light that gives hope and a balm that brings healing in just the ways you need.

God bless you on your journey.

DRAW NEAR IN FAITH

Come close to God, and God will come close to you.

JAMES 4:8 NLT

When faced with a loss, whether of a loved one or a long-held dream, it's easy and natural to feel alone and abandoned and ask, "Why would God allow such pain and disappointment? If He is so good and since He could have stopped it, why didn't He?" During those times, it's no fault of any of us to think, *I thought You loved me, Lord. How could You let this happen?* These are times when we analyze and pick apart all that led to our fragmented state, which eventually leads to a final crossroad: Will we walk away from God, or will we continue to seek His face and draw near in faith?

According to today's promise, He longs for us to come—just as we are, without conditions. He is waiting to receive our broken hearts, our broken dreams, even our broken faith. He, and only He, can love our shattered pieces back into something that is beautiful and whole, if only we will let Him. Will you draw close to God today? If you do, He will come close to you.

Father, it is hard to understand why You would allow such pain in my life. I thought You were a God of goodness and love, yet I feel crushed and confused. This is a time when I come to You in sheer faith because I don't see You through yesterday's lens. I come to You with all hope that Your Spirit will overtake me and pull me into Your arms of comfort because I need it. I need to know and trust that You're with me and that You are in control. So please be with me now and help me through this day.

IN JESUS' NAME. AMEN.

HIS HOLY EMBRACE

Faithful love and truth will join together;
righteousness and peace will embrace.

PSALM 85:10

When we're down in the deep recesses of pain, it's natural to feel alone because no one else on the earth knows or understands exactly what we're feeling or why. Sometimes we don't even know ourselves; we just know that life has stopped and doing the simplest task is like climbing a mountain that doesn't end. It's in those times when God's faithful love reaches up from the earth and His righteousness and peace look down from the heavens, and we are caught in His Divine embrace.

The sweet spot of an embrace is the chest, where two hearts touch and beat together in rhythmic harmony, if only for a moment. So just imagine the tidal wave of love and comfort God sends from His heart directly into ours when we turn to Him and say, "Yes, I want You and need You, Lord. Please hold me throughout this day." And He says, "Come into My arms, and I will."

Father, I need Your embrace today
deep within my soul, for the comfort
and hope that only You can give. I simply
can't do life without You being within me
and beside me to steady my heart and calm
my nerves. I long to hear Your whispers
of love for the assurance I need that You are
with me and that You care. Your presence
is life-giving to my soul, so please help me
to rise and receive the love You have to give.
Let it work in me a new light of hope
and healing I wouldn't otherwise have.
It's because of You that I live.

IN JESUS' NAME. AMEN.

13

TIME TO MOURN

---

*The Lord said to Samuel, "How long will you mourn
for Saul, since I have rejected him as king over Israel?
Fill your horn with oil and be on your way."*

I SAMUEL 16:1 NIV

Saul had reigned for forty-two years over Israel, and the time had come that the Lord would have permanently established him as king. But Saul disobeyed, so the Lord would not appoint him. Samuel was then given the unpleasant task of telling Saul that the Lord had rejected him, which was very difficult for Samuel to do. He had been with Saul from the beginning of his reign, so learning such bad news and being given the commission to deliver it broke Samuel's heart.

After the mission was accomplished, Samuel was so downcast that he mourned. God's Word doesn't say how long he mourned, just that God knew why he mourned, and that He gave Samuel the time and space to do so. This is very telling of the importance of grieving. Even though we don't always understand the road or the process grief takes us on, it's vital that we submit to it for a time and let God do His work in us until He says otherwise.

Father, I'm so grateful for Your grace and mercy as I simply grieve. I know You understand the depth of what I'm going through even more than I do. Thank You for letting me be still in my pain and for comforting me in the process. I trust You and love You for the tender care You show to me each day.

IN JESUS' NAME. AMEN.

BE STILL

"Be still, and know that I am God!"
PSALM 46:10 NLT

When living in the clutches of pain and feeling lost in our circumstances, it's only natural to want to do something, take something, go somewhere, or be with someone to get our minds off our hurt or make it go away altogether. But doing, taking, going are all actions that go against what God often wants and tells us to do . . . to be still and know that He is God. This means we are to quiet our minds and acknowledge who He is in relation to ourselves and the troubled condition of our hearts. When we do, the greatness of His majesty comes into view and His peace that passes all understanding is ours in abundance. Only in knowing He is God are we able to release with all trust what we cannot control into the hands of the One who is in total control.

In His mercy, God comes down into the recesses of our valleys to comfort and give hope. But He is also far above the details that limit our view of what He is doing and how He will restore all that's been lost. And we must trust that. He is God, and He is good.

Father, it's hard to be still. My flesh wants to do whatever it can to ease my pain and use my own logic to make sense of my circumstances. Please surround me with Your presence and help me to stop my mind from whirling and my body from striving. I want to rest in You. I want to remember that You are God, and You are over all— both the good and the bad.

IN YOUR SAVING GRACE, I PRAY.
AMEN.

THE NEXT COMMON THING

[Elijah] said, "I have had enough! Lord, take my life, for I'm no better than my ancestors." Then he lay down and slept under the broom tree. Suddenly, an angel touched him. The angel told him, "Get up and eat."

I KINGS 19:4-5

Just like Elijah, unexpected turns in life can leave us wanting to lie down, curl up, and die. We become so exhausted that getting out of bed is not an option—there's nothing left but a pull to stay down, and the thought of working toward life as we knew it is overwhelming. These are times when working on *anything* is better left for a future time. Simply doing the next smallest act will bring the biggest reward, and that is merely to get up and eat.

Our bodies need the basics—such as food and water. Our minds need the basics—such as simply knowing that Jesus loves us. Our spirits need truth and life from God's Word—such as knowing that He is with us. Sometimes life needs to be that simple, and that's okay. Our goal for each day is to do the next basic thing for as long as we need. God understands.

*Father, I'm so weak and lacking in desire
to do anything except lie down and sleep.
I need rest, I need sleep, I need for my mind
to be still and soak in some quiet. Help me
to do the next thing by caring for my basic
needs. Give me strength to feed my body.
Give me Your Spirit to feed my soul. Give
me Your presence to comfort my wounds.
Give me the time and space I need right
now to simply rest. I need You, Lord—
be with me now.*

IN JESUS' NAME. AMEN.

HE HAS A PLAN FOR YOU

The student is not above the teacher,
nor a servant above his master.

MATTHEW 10:24 NIV

When one's heart is downcast, it's difficult to think about anything except the surrounding brokenness and loss; trying to crawl out of the mire can be all-consuming. Just imagine how all-consumed Jesus was as He prepared to receive brutal beatings and be nailed to a cross. If He had to endure such pain in order to fulfill His Father's bigger plan, we, too, will be faced with times of pain and challenges. We simply aren't above it. Knowing this doesn't necessarily ease our pain, but accepting whatever God allows in our lives—the good and the bad—is the first step toward the peace that comes out of pure and holy trust in Him.

From a worldly view, Jesus' death could be seen as a horrible mistake. From a heavenly view, His death was the most precious and ultimate gift God had to give. He had a plan for His Son all along, and He has a plan for your life as well.

Father, as much as I hurt, as hard as it is,
help me to take my eyes off my loss
and remember what You went through
to sacrifice Your own Son for me. There is
no doubt that You understand the depth
of what I'm going through, and that brings
me comfort. Be with me this day and instill
in me the strength to give thanks to You—
for the sacrifice You made and for how
I can live with the simple knowledge
of Your presence and holiness in my life.

IN JESUS' NAME. AMEN.

HE IS EVER-PRESENT

*I am convinced that nothing can ever separate us
from God's love. Neither death nor life, neither angels
nor demons, neither our fears for today nor our worries
about tomorrow—not even the powers of hell
can separate us from God's love.*

ROMANS 8:38 NLT

It's so much easier to keep going through life when we know we are not alone. And sometimes, even though there are times when we feel alone and secluded from the world and those around us, we are never alone or removed from the holy presence of God. What a comfort that is ours when we truly embrace this and remember that no matter what, we are loved, thought of, and prayed for through the Spirit. Christ Himself intercedes for us when we can't speak; His Spirit is our healing balm from within that no outside force can diminish. He guards us, loves us, and looks after our every need as we work through the details of each day.

Press into Him now, and simply enjoy the fact that He is your closest companion, and He is actively and lovingly praying, moving, and working on your behalf.

*Lord, thank You for Your promise
to always be with me and that nothing
can separate You from my life and my
heart. I welcome You with full gratitude
that You are watching over me and all
that I face. Help me to keep my hope
in You and not in any results I desire
or tasks I need to accomplish. You are
my way, my truth, and my life—
nothing compares to the presence of Your
tender touch of love that I feel.*

IN YOUR SWEET NAME, I PRAY.
AMEN.

HE'S IN OUR TRIALS

*After you have suffered a little while, our God, who is
full of kindness through Christ, will give you His eternal
glory. He personally will come and pick you up, and set
you firmly in place, and make you stronger than ever.*

I PETER 5:10 TLB

Just imagine a child who has fallen and become overwhelmed with her surroundings to the point of tears and immobility. Then suddenly, out of love and concern, her father rushes in, swoops her up in his arms, and takes her to safety and shelter. This is exactly what our heavenly Father does when we're weakened by pain and don't know how to keep going on our own. He doesn't keep us from experiencing painful trials—for in them, our faith is made "stronger than ever"—but He does meet us and help us to higher ground, where our feet are secure and we're able to walk once again on the road of righteousness that He has paved.

Just as the children of Israel were led through great trials of slavery and eventually out of captivity, we as children of God are not left, but rather we are led through the calamities of this day into safe pastures for His keeping. All glory be to Him.

*Father, help me to remember that I am
not alone. Help me to remember that,
as much as I hurt, You are doing a great
work in me. Help me to remember that You
are the Lifter of my soul and the Keeper
of my very life. I trust that You will
help me through the grief that surrounds
and fills my every fiber. Your strength will
be my strength. Your hope will be my hope.
Your kindness will cover me with the break
of each new day through to the setting of
the sun. You are so good, and I am grateful
for Your promises that keep my hope alive.*

ALL GLORY BE TO YOU. AMEN.

BLESSINGS IN RECEIVING

God has put the body together. . . . So if one member
suffers, all the members suffer with it; if one member
is honored, all the members rejoice with it.
I CORINTHIANS 12:24–26

In the wake of tragedy, it is necessary to get alone with God in order to hear His voice and receive the comfort only He can give, but it's also good not to be alone for long. It's a time to allow other members of your family and church and neighborhood into your world, no matter how messy it is, and let them minister to your heart in ways no one else can. There is blessing in receiving help in the home—in the kitchen, in the laundry room, in the layers of dust—and in all the moments when life doesn't stop just because you have. And what's truly special are the moments when others simply stop to suffer with you in your hardship as well as rejoice over the milestones of healing. Then, as you regain your strength and momentum to live again, it'll be your turn to do the same for the next person.

May we all walk in God's plan with grace and humility for all the suffering souls.

Father, thank You for those who have suffered with me, thank You for those who have reached out and helped me during the days and nights when I've not been able to move. Thank You for each step toward healing I've made and for the joyful moments of encouragement and kinship when others have reached out to me. I'm thankful not to be alone, except when I'm with You in the silent moments of the day, when Your voice and presence is all I want to hear and feel. Your love reaching down, Your love expressed through others, is a true blessing.

IN YOUR PRECIOUS NAME, I PRAY.
AMEN.

OPEN THE DOOR
TO YOUR HEART

He will rescue the poor when they cry to him;
he will help the oppressed,
who have no one to defend them.

PSALM 72:12 NLT

God is constantly with us, watching over us, and waiting to hear from the cries of our hearts. He wants us to speak frankly and truthfully about the troubles we face and the emotions we feel. He waits for the door of our hearts to be opened wide in order to fully deliver the portion we need to sustain each day we live. If we need a new couch to sit on, our front door must be completely open in order to move the piece from our front porch into the heart of the living room where we dwell. Or if we need a rescue team to come into our home to help in an emergency, the door must be opened wide for them to enter with all their equipment that aids them.

Keep the door of your heart open as wide as you can and cry out to God with abandon. He is the ultimate Helper, who has no bounds as to what He can do, and He wants to be that Helper for you.

Lord, I cry to You from the depths of my heart and look to You to bring me help. I need comfort, I need healing, I need a hand to hold mine as I navigate through life right now. I open my heart to You and claim Your promises to rescue me, hold me, guard me, and sustain me. I claim all of them for myself today and trust You to be my near-and-present Savior of hope. Nothing compares to the secure and solid rest I have in Your love.

IN YOUR GREAT NAME, I PRAY.
AMEN.

DO NOT BE AFRAID

Do not fear, for I am with you; do not be afraid,
for I am your God. I will strengthen you; I will help you;
I will hold on to you with My righteous right hand.

ISAIAH 41:10

Being with a partner, then suddenly finding yourself alone can be frightening. Whether because of abandonment, divorce, or loss through death, being suddenly alone can shake your identity and daily life as you knew it, down to the smallest detail. You're faced with the presence of absence, and this opens the door to vulnerability. Where there is vulnerability, there is an enemy ushering fear into your thoughts and actions.

Our loving Lord knows this, and that is why He addresses it head-on and clearly states that we should not be afraid—ever. He promises to help us when we need it—we are not alone. He holds on to us with His righteous right hand, and He will not let us go. He is bigger and stronger, smarter and more effective than any amount of human logic we could muster from a downcast and broken time. He loves and He cares.

Father, I can't help but feel shaken and wonder who I am right now. Everything's changed, and what used to feel ordinary and routine takes concerted thought and effort to figure out what I'm doing. You tell me not to be afraid, but I confess I struggle with fear and worry, and I lack the confidence I had only a short time ago. I cling to Your promise that You will strengthen and help me, because I really need that right now. I believe You've got me covered and You won't steer me wrong as I navigate back into the identity and purpose I know I have in You.

I LOVE YOU WITH ALL MY HEART.
AMEN.

BE WHAT YOU NEED TO BE

I love You, LORD; You are my strength.

PSALM 18:1 NLT

When you are going through a valley of sadness, there can be a daily struggle of saying you're fine when you aren't. There can be internal pressure to wear a smile as you pass by people around you when, deep down, you don't want to smile, you don't want to ask how they are doing, you don't want to pretend you're okay when you're not. Your only strength is God's portion on your life, one moment at a time.

But when you get down to what really matters during difficult days, there is the truth that it's okay not to be okay. It's okay to be real, to feel vulnerable, and to speak honestly instead of trying to hide behind a false pretense of happiness. Reflecting on the outside what lies inside is not only freeing, but it presents the opportunity for another caring soul to walk into your world and bring you the pure and sincere comfort you need.

God gave us our emotions not to hide them but to let them be what they need to be until we're ready to say that we are okay.

Lord, I'm so thankful to know that You understand how hard it is for me to be around others and to act as though I'm okay when I'm not. My heart is broken, yet I don't want to stand out. At the same time, this is not a time to cater to any expectations of being fine and well. I need and want to be honest about what I'm really going through and that I'm not okay right now. Instead of fighting any pressure to hurry up and heal, help me to accept what I feel and allow myself the grace I need to come up out of the depths in my own time. You are my strength today and tomorrow and the next day until I can stand once again in the full measure of being whole.

I LOVE YOU, AND I LEAN
INTO YOUR STRENGTH. AMEN.

HIS BANNER OF LOVE

You have shown your people desperate times. . . .
But for those who fear You, You have raised a banner
to be unfurled against the bow.

King Solomon would say that living in desperate times is nothing new under the sun—Jesus even tells us to expect them. And whether or not you are in a desperate time, you're likely experiencing difficulty that is beyond your ability to control or possibly even comprehend. This is why it matters to the greatest degree that we know our God is full of compassion and mercy. He is grieved when we hurt, and as our prayers and pleas rise up to His listening ear, His banner of love unfurls over the details of our circumstances in such a way that we cannot help but be encouraged.

Soak in His presence today; claim His strength as your own; abide in His covering of love with abandon; and know that you are not alone. He cares for you and your life down to the smallest detail.

Lord, knowing You are with me gives me the courage I need to face another day. Hold me up and help me to keep walking toward the victory that is mine when I abide in You and claim Your promises throughout Your Word. Fill me with Your peace that passes all understanding, because I don't understand so much of why life is the way it is. Keep me from falling prey to the temptation to give up. Help me to remember Your covering of love and the protection I have as I walk in it. I cling to Your steady hand today and praise You for Your faithfulness and provision.

IN JESUS' NAME, I PRAY.
AMEN.

YOU ARE . . .

After experiencing loss of any kind, there's one thing we all do that makes the process of healing very hard, and that's continually looking at the past and what could have been. When we dwell on what isn't anymore, it's as though a veil blocks our steps toward new beginnings that God has in store. Taking time to grieve what isn't is vital for moving on, but at the same time, it's good to remember that what no longer is, isn't a stamp of who you aren't now. There must be a renewing of your mind in order to fully grasp onto and live in the truth for your life today.

And right now, this very day, you are loved. You are a precious child of God. You are fearfully and wonderfully made. You are part of a bigger, sovereign plan. You are able, through the power of Christ in you, to do all that He has called you to do. You are priceless. You are not forgotten. You are in the presence of almighty God, and you are in His hands.

*Father, help me to look at and claim
all that I am in You. Help me to heal
from what no longer is and take another
step forward into a new and holy plan
that You have for me now. Help me
to completely trust in who You say
that I am, not in what I think I'm not.
In You, I am whole and complete.
Now help me to truly embrace this
and walk in victory today.*

IN JESUS' NAME AND POWER, I PRAY.
AMEN.

TREASURE UP

Mary was treasuring up all these things in her heart and meditating on them.

LUKE 2:19

Often when your heart is burdened, your mind won't turn off. Thoughts about the whys and what ifs can replay over and over, and before you know it, you've spent thirty minutes rabbit-trailing down different scenarios, only to find your thoughts in the same place they began. This can be frustrating and futile when all you want are answers or an understanding of why.

The best way to capture your thoughts and steer them in a positive and peaceful direction is to do what Mary did: Treasure up God's truths and meditate on them. This means taking a promise from God's Word and choosing to dwell on what it means for you. As Oswald Chambers says, "Let God's truth work into you by immersing yourself in it, not by worrying into it."*

Will you commit to finding a verse that speaks to you, and allow yourself to truly rest in its truth as your own?

My Utmost for His Highest, copyright © 1992 by Oswald Chambers Publications Association, Ltd.

Dear Lord, I need Your help with reining in my thoughts. It's hard to settle my mind because I want answers, and I want them now. I want to change the bad that's happened to me. I want to do away with the control my pain has over me. Will You please lead me to a verse that will help me today? I want to learn it, claim it, and abide in it. I simply want more of You in my mind to bring the comfort and peace I so long for.

IN YOUR SWEET NAME, I PRAY.
AMEN.

NO APOLOGIES

"How long are you going to stay drunk?" Eli asked her. . . .
Hannah responded, . . . "I'm not drunk. I'm depressed.
I'm pouring out my heart to the Lord. . . . I was praying
like this because I've been troubled and tormented."

I SAMUEL 1:14-16 GW

Even though depression is a normal stage of suffering loss, it can be an ugly companion that pours sadness into the places where joy used to be. To top it off, when others see you depressed, there can be a misunderstanding about your behavior. In the same way Eli thought Hannah was drunk, family, friends, and neighbors can mistake or misread your actions in ways they take personally rather than see into the core of your struggle.

Just as Hannah had to clarify to Eli that she was depressed, there will be times when you may have to do the same. Remember one thing Hannah didn't do: She didn't apologize. She was expressing the truth of her pain to her Father in heaven, and there is no place for apology in that. He wants us to come just as we are. He wants the truth of our pain to rise into His loving hands, no matter what others may think.

Father, I don't want to hold back.
I want You to see all the hurt in my heart
and take it from me. I need Your light
and Your love to bless me and keep me.
Guard me from what others think
and help me to remain solely focused on
Your compassion that surrounds me
and Your Spirit that consoles me.

IN YOU ALONE I TRUST AND PRAY.
AMEN.

HE IS WORKING

We know that all things work together
for the good of those who love God,
who are called according to His purpose.

ROMANS 8:28

While under the weight of grief, the momentum of ordinary life can diminish to the point where everything moves in slow motion. Sometimes there isn't *any* motion—our hearts, our minds, our bodies come to a complete stop. And thank goodness they do, because at that point, the capacity to function with any clarity can be gone. It's even tempting to fall into a frame of mind that doesn't care about anything, which can be unsettling. What are we to do when this happens? How can we keep enough hope alive that we are able to get up instead of give in to the stronghold of pain?

Paul doesn't say, "We think" or "We imagine" that God works all things together for our good. He says, "We *know*." It's a solid truth that we—including you—can hold on to without waver. He *will* at some point work the situation you're in now for your good and for His glory.

42

Lord, it is so hard to see how anything
good can come out of my circumstances.
The only way I can process this promise
of working them for my good is to simply
believe, even if by only a thread. Help me
to hold on to that, even if it means for one
day, one minute, at a time. I've got
to have hope that all is not lost and that,
in time, You will work the goodness
of Your love and Your purpose for my life
into something miraculous. I love You
and trust You to be over my life, and that
gives me great comfort.

IN YOUR PRECIOUS SON'S NAME,
I PRAY. AMEN.

HE IS TRUSTWORTHY

You saw in the wilderness how the Lord your God carried you as a man carries his son all along the way you traveled until you reached this place. But in spite of this you did not trust the Lord your God, who went before you on the journey to seek out a place for you to camp.

DEUTERONOMY 1:31-33

When riding the torrents that grief and loss can bring, a vital lifeline for staying afloat is trust. But finding a true source to trust in can be hard to do. That's because we so often put our trust in other people, which, at some point, leads to disappointment. And in all the hurt and disillusionment, we often project our distrust in the people who've hurt us onto God. It's something we do without consciously thinking about it, and it can be a challenge to undo until we are deliberate in our thoughts.

Looking back, what is the evidence of God's goodness in your life? Do you see Him taking care of you time and again? Do you see the touches of His love that are special only to you? After gathering all the proof, it becomes obvious: He alone is trustworthy. He is *the* lifeline to hold on to today, tonight, and again tomorrow.

*Father, I'm sorry I've not trusted You
to the fullest extent You deserve. When
I remember the countless times You've
provided, You've given me strength,
and You've led my way, I can see
insurmountable evidence of Your goodness
to me time and again. I lean into
and hold on to my trust in You now.
Help me to stay focused on all
You've done and to believe in all
the good You will do in my future.*

I TRUST YOU, JESUS. AMEN.

HE IS WITH YOU

[The two disciples] were deep in conversation,
going over all these things that had happened.
In the middle of their talk and questions,
Jesus came up and walked along with them.
But they were not able to recognize who He was.

LUKE 24:14-16 THE MESSAGE

Three days after Jesus' death and resurrection, two disciples were walking together, talking about what had happened. They were discouraged and probably feeling downcast and abandoned by the Savior. And then, Jesus "came up and walked with them." The men didn't recognize Him, but He was there, very much a part of their conversation and journey. They invited Him to spend the evening, which He did, and only then did they realize who He was.

Jesus had been with them all along. He walked their same road of distress; He participated in the discussion; He stayed with them until they finally recognized His presence. And, in the same way, Jesus is walking with you now. He hears every word, every prayer, and He feels your heartache and struggle.

Lord Jesus, I trust that You are with me
now, and that You are very much a part
of what I'm going through. I want You to
speak into my heart and help me navigate
through this journey I'm on. I'm grateful
to know You are near regardless of how
I feel. The truth is, You are with me,
You won't leave, and I need You more
than ever today and tomorrow
and the next day. Thank You, Lord,
for the comfort this brings.

I LOVE YOU AND PRAY THIS
IN YOUR NAME. AMEN.

CAUGHT BY THE SPIRIT

You keep track of all my sorrows.
You have collected all my tears in Your bottle.
You have recorded each one in Your book.

PSALM 56:8 NLT

Reality is, many people are uncomfortable around someone who grieves. There can often be an awkwardness of what to say or do. Sometimes others even avoid us altogether in order to walk around their own discomfort with sadness. But where people fall short, God compensates for their lack. He comes toward us in our pain, He infuses His Spirit of mercy right at the point where others leave off. He sees our tears, He collects them in His bottle.

There's an unexplainable peace in knowing that our pleas and our cries don't go out into the nothingness of space. Instead, they are caught by the Spirit's hand, gathered together, and lovingly placed at the foot of His throne where He keeps track of our journeys. Each day, He watches and knows every step and thought and circumstance we find ourselves in, and He receives them unto Himself. It is a gift beyond description to know that we have such a loving and caring God.

Father, it's hard enough to carry my grief,
but it hurts even more that others seem
more distant than usual. I'm so grateful
to know that You are with me and that
whatever I say or feel, You are listening
and You understand. I trust You to hold
my aching heart in Your hands and that
You won't let it go. Where people fail me,
I look to You to sustain me. Where others
are absent, I relish in Your presence and
care. I know I'll get through this season
with Your help and Your love.
Carry me now, and don't let me go.

IN JESUS' NAME. AMEN.

JESUS' UNMISTAKEN TOUCH

*What a wonderful God we have—He is the Father
of our Lord Jesus Christ, the source of every mercy,
and the one who so wonderfully comforts
and strengthens us in our hardships and trials.*

II CORINTHIANS 1:3 TLB

There are times when difficult days, challenging months, and long, dark seasons envelop us to the point we can barely think. Living one day at a time turns into functioning one minute at a time.

But during these times when words are few, we still have a voice, and we still have a prayer. Jesus steps in with an unmistaken touch. He is there in the midst of the trouble, carrying us and keeping us until our hearts can once again beat on their own. It's what He loves to do—embrace each of us with His tender, loving care and escort us into wholeness once again.

In His gentle mercy and compassion, let Him hold you now.

*Lord of compassion, I'm grateful
for Your presence and Your healing touch.
You lift me up when I can't rise, You carry
me when I'm not able to move, You cup
Your hands around the shattered pieces
of my heart, and You simply are so I can
simply be. Please don't leave—stay through
the season of nights that are ahead.
Be my hope for a future I can't see
and a purpose for a cause I've lost.*

HOLD ON TO ME NOW. AMEN.

LEAN BACK
AGAINST JESUS

[John] leaned back against Jesus . . .

JOHN 13:25

John, Jesus' disciple and friend, was reclined next to Jesus after eating a meal, then he leaned back against Jesus. This is an act that takes complete trust and assurance that it's okay to touch, let alone touch the Savior of the world. It speaks volumes about the closeness of their relationship because John felt safe within the realm of their friendship, as well as at peace, because he knew Jesus would keep him from falling. John loved and trusted Him within a deep and abiding connection. Jesus obviously felt the same.

It is the same for us when we recline our hearts and spend time in His presence. He is there when we can stand, but He is also there to catch us when we aren't able to uphold ourselves from the burden of our grief. He is able and willing to take on the weight that a downcast spirit brings and listen to our cries for as long as we need. What a friend we have in Jesus.

Lord Jesus, I love You and trust You.
I want to lean against You now and tell You
all about the way I'm feeling today. I didn't
know life could be so hard, but I know
You understand. You are my Savior
and my Friend, who holds me up so I'm
able to endure and persevere in ways
I never thought I could. Thank You for
Your presence; thank You for remaining my
help and support through each and every
moment of this season. Your grace and love
are sufficient for me, and I am grateful.

IN YOUR GREAT NAME, I PRAY.
AMEN.

WHEN WORDS
DON'T COME

*The Spirit also helps us in our weakness, because
we do not know what to pray for as we should,
but the Spirit himself intercedes for us
with inexpressible groanings.*

ROMANS 8:26

Charles Spurgeon said, "Wordless groans are often prayers that God cannot refuse." And when grief-stricken hearts are void of words, there can be nothing but groans with stretches of silence and sobs in the mix. This is when Paul says that the Spirit of Jesus Himself comes in and prays on our behalf to our one, true Source of comfort—our Abba Father. They are golden bowls of incense set before the King (see Revelation 5:8), calling on His compassion and strength to carry us through yet another day.

When we don't have the words, Jesus does, and He speaks them freely for our benefit and blessing. We can rest assured they've been sent and received, and they will not return void.

Jesus, I call to You now from the spirit of my heart. I know not what to pray—words just don't come. I'm at a loss and only know that I need Your help. Please hold me up, carry me through, hear my cries, and heal my heart before I fall apart. Please take this pain that I feel and replace it with Your strength for today. I want to rest in You, trusting that You are with me now and that You hear me. If I have nothing else, let Your compassion be my closest friend. You are my Sustainer and Healer, and I take comfort in knowing You speak to the Father on my behalf. I love You and thank You for loving me.

IN YOUR PRECIOUS NAME.
AMEN.

DON'T BE ANXIOUS

Don't be anxious about tomorrow. God will take care of your tomorrow too. Live one day at a time.

MATTHEW 6:34 TLB

Divorce proceedings, bills far greater than your bank balance, loss of work and the identity you had with it—these and many more situations are very real joy-stealers that can bring their own grief to a recipient's heart. Dreams once held close are destroyed within an instant, and they can all lead into a whirl of worry about tomorrow with the questions "What if?" and "What am I going to do?"

And to this, Jesus said, "Live one day at a time." Sometimes all we can do is to live one step at a time, and this is okay. "Our main business is not to see what lies dimly at a distance, but to do what lies clearly at hand."* Tomorrow is a distance just far enough away to cloud our view—today is the day we are to keep our thoughts, our actions, and our trust in God with the hope that what we do today will benefit our tomorrow. And what's needed for tomorrow, God promises to provide (see Isaiah 58:11). We simply must believe it.

*Thomas Carlyle

*Lord God, You know what I am facing—
not only my circumstances, but the level
of trust and faith I have in You. You say
not to worry about tomorrow, but it's hard
not to. I need Your help to stay focused on
today and to hold on to my belief in Your
power as well as Your sovereignty over my
life. Help me to release tomorrow into Your
hands and seek Your wisdom and strength
as I go through this day, which is a gift
from You. I love You and hold on to
the love You have for me.*

IN JESUS' NAME. AMEN.

LORD, HELP ME!

*When [Peter] looked down at the waves churning
beneath his feet, he lost his nerve and started to sink.
He cried, "Master, save me!" Jesus didn't hesitate.
He reached down and grabbed his hand.*

MATTHEW 14:29–31 THE MESSAGE

When the high winds of life whirl around us, it's only natural to put our focus on its power and imagine the destruction it's about to cause. It's no different from watching news channels running continuous live videos of hurricane-force gusts causing trees to snap and rooftops to lift completely off buildings. In the aftermath, it's impossible not to venture outside to see the damage and evaluate the cost of repair, which alone can be overwhelming.

This is when it's tempting to lose hope and think all is lost, but there is hope. There is nothing beyond God's ability to repair and redeem, but the key to really believing this is to hold on to that truth—not our circumstances. Just as Jesus didn't hesitate to reach down and keep Peter from sinking, He won't delay reaching into your life and grabbing your hand. He is just a cry away.

Lord, help me! Sometimes I struggle not to feel overwhelmed as though I'm sinking into an ocean too big for me to get out of. Please grab my hand and hold me close in a place that is safe and still. Keep me on solid ground, where my faith remains intact and my hope won't waver. I believe You are still in control and that You will help me through my circumstances. I trust in You and rest in Your peace, and I thank You for the power You give to get through this day in victory.

IN YOUR NAME, I PRAY. AMEN.

EYES ON THE PRIZE

I focus on this one thing: Forgetting the past and looking forward to what lies ahead, I press on to reach the end of the race and receive the heavenly prize for which God, through Christ Jesus, is calling us.

PHILIPPIANS 3:13–14 NLT

Grief is so unpredictable. One day you can seem to be making progress out from under its weight, and the next day there doesn't seem to be any escape. It's hard to lift your sights out of the present moment and see what new life is ahead. Paul understood this all too well—he struggled to forget his years of persecuting, even killing, believers for following the very Christ who had saved his life. Yet he found a way to keep moving forward: He worked to forget his past and to keep looking at the prize that lay ahead. His prize was the heavenly prize we *all* have through our relationship with Jesus.

So, when an earthly prize that used to fill your heart is no longer here, you always have a heavenly one to live for and claim as your own. See it, fixate on it, and let it be your focus that lies ahead.

Lord, help me to remember that,
even though part of my prize in life
is now gone, I always have an eternal,
heavenly prize to look forward to. Help me
to fix my gaze on that promise and be filled
with renewed strength to live another day
to the fullest. Help me to hear Your daily
call to rise and claim the victory that is
mine when I live in the fullness of Your
grace. I need You for my very breath of life,
and I trust that You will keep my head and
sights lifted so my hope is always in view.

ALL PRAISE BE TO YOU. AMEN.

LOOK UP

I lift up my eyes to the mountains—
where does my help come from?
My help comes from the Lord,
the Maker of heaven and earth.
He will not let your foot slip.

PSALM 121:1-3 NIV

We don't know what this psalmist was facing to need the kind of supernatural help he called upon when he wrote this verse, but it's clear there was nothing on his level of understanding that looked hopeful. So his eyes looked up to the highest point of reference they could find: mountaintops.

Whether literally or figuratively, it is there in the heights where a bigger perspective of what we're going through is seen, and there is no other source who can dwell in those heights except our loving God. And from there, He sees you now. His help coming down in your life today is the same help that came down over two thousand years ago to save the world. His hand is on your life the same way it was on this psalmist, who clearly believed in His almighty power. Hopefully, you do too.

*O Lord, I look up to the heavens
and believe You will deliver the help
that I need. I trust that You hear this cry
from my heart and that Your hand
will keep me from falling. Even though
I can't see clearly around me, I know
and trust that You can and that Your help
is but a breath away. I want to rest
and take refuge in that today.*

ALL GLORY BE TO YOU. AMEN.

HE IS YAHWEH, HE IS HERE

*Even when walking through the dark valley of death
I will not be afraid, for You are close beside me,
guarding, guiding all the way.*

PSALM 23:4 TLB

Just as Jesus prayed for the cup of crucifixion to pass, we often want God to remove the pressures and pain we face in our lives. Sometimes He will, but there are defining times when He won't, and it becomes clear that the only way to navigate our course is through. But in His love and merciful grace, He promises to go through those times with us. He remains in the very core of the wreckage, where He provides exactly what is needed to sustain our beating hearts.

He is Yahweh and He holds our very lives in His hands to do as He wills. Through it all, each day can boil down to either putting our hope in this fallen world and what it has to offer or putting it in the One who created us all with a heavenly purpose, which He is orchestrating to fulfill this very moment. Sometimes it can be a daily choice to make over and over, and that's okay. In His infinite love, He understands.

Father, I choose You to guide me through this day and restore my broken heart with the true and lasting hope that only You can give. Hold me, carry me, cover my life, speak to me, and remind me that You are Yahweh. You are the Creator and Sustainer of the forces of the universe, and yet You know me, and You dearly love me. I hold on to that today with all that I have.

PRAISE YOU, JESUS. AMEN.

HOPE IN HIM

Be strong, and let your heart be courageous,
all you who put your hope in the LORD.

PSALM 31:24

Suffering, no matter its source, does one thing to us all: It depletes us of strength. Sleep deprivation, stress-filled circumstances, anxiety, worry—they literally diminish our energy and alter our ability to function normally and think clearly. All this at a time when we need our strength the most.

But this psalm is the perfect antidote for our times of weakness, and it tells us to put our hope in the Lord. When we do, the result is that His strength and His courage become our own. With hope in Him, we are renewed with power and girded with valor to overcome the obstacles that sadness brings for the duration we need. Not that we'll go from one extreme to the other, but that His provision will be all-sufficient for each day as we place our hope above the dark clouds into the presence of His light.

Lord, I am weak. I am exhausted.
I don't see clearly to know what to do with
the sadness that's all around. I need a ray
of light, a beam of hope from my heart,
lifted up and fixed on You. I gladly soak
in Your strength for today and draw from
the courage that You give in order to walk
on solid ground and remain steadfast
in spirit. You are my light, my hope,
my comfort, and my anchor for staying
strong so I can do what I need to do today.
Because of You, I live. Because of Your
love, I have hope. Because of Your strength,
I am able.

ALL GLORY BE TO YOU. AMEN.

OUR MATTERS
ARE IN HIS HANDS

---

*But You Yourself have seen trouble and grief,
observing it in order to take the matter into Your hands.*

PSALM 10:14

How much does grief weigh? How many pounds of pressure can our feeble hearts withstand before giving way to the heaviness that presses in around us? Enough to immobilize even the most stalwart of souls; enough to push the very breath out of our lungs and resist our attempts at filling them again; and enough to reveal that we are no match for carrying the weight in our own strength. The good news is, we don't have to.

God, through His resurrecting power, gladly takes our matters into His own hands and resuscitates our hope. But there's even more. He is also the lifter of our heavy heads (Psalm 3:3), the healer of our broken hearts (Psalm 147:3), and the sustainer of His righteous children, enough so that they will never be moved (Psalm 55:22)—and never is a long time.

God knew we'd face grievous times, and it's why He makes it clear that He is here to help and to save.

Father, the weight of heaviness I feel inside is sometimes too much to bear. Please take it from me. Please heal my heart and firmly plant my feet on solid ground that won't give way. I need Your strength; I need Your power; I need Your loving arms fixed around me, so I'll know You're with me with every step I take. Take my life into Your own hands and allow me to rest in Your presence. With You, I can go on. With You, I can endure. With You, my hope is strong for the time when my heart is once again filled with Your joy and I can praise You for all the goodness You have done.

IN JESUS' NAME. AMEN.

GOD'S SILENCE,
OUR STILLNESS

When suffering of any kind hits and we go to God with our brokenness, sometimes the wait to hear from Him can be as painful as the situation we're facing. But God's silence does not mean His absence. He is all in, around, before, and behind, and sometimes it takes the still of His silence to get us to be still as well so we can hear the whispers of His presence. It's hard to be still because that's when we feel our pain the most. But the more we put off the pain, the more we put off our healing, and He knows that.

We want the quickest route up out of our valley floors—God's aim is for us to be whole through the work He does in our healing. Just as a child must be still for a doctor to examine and fix a wound, we must be still to let God in and apply His soothing balm right where it's needed. We must take time to be still and feel.

Father, I need Your presence, I need to hear
Your voice, I need Your comfort right now.
I am hurting and trusting that You are
with me even though You seem absent.
Your Word says that You are near
the brokenhearted (Psalm 34:18),
so I claim that now, in faith, and cling to
Your nearness and the peace it gives.
Be with me, help me, as I go through
the pain that's all around; heal my heart
and give me strength as I go through
this day that You have given.

IN YOUR LOVING ARMS I WILL REST.
AMEN.

HIS EVERYDAY TOUCH

*Praise the Lᴏʀᴅ, for He has shown me
the wonders of His unfailing love.*

PSALM 31:21 NLT

When our hearts are hurting, it may feel at times that we are alone, but we're not. There are sources all around that God provides for us to reach for and hold on to that can bring comfort in varying degrees. Of course, His Word is living and active and is filled with comfort that only the Savior can give. But sometimes He comforts through something as simple as the happy greeting of a dog or the purr of a cat. It could be a child's hug or the wave of a neighbor. Another time it could be a phone call or text from a friend or the prayer of a pastor.

God leans into our lives through all kinds of avenues to reach into our hearts and instill the comfort He knows we need. He knows and He cares, and He is gracious enough to reinforce this through our everyday lives. So be on the lookout for how He will touch your heart today.

Lord, help me to see all the ways You reach out to Me and to receive them as the holy and gentle ways You show Your love. I need them, I want them, and I don't take them for granted. Thank You for loving me down to the smallest detail in ways I don't expect but clearly know are of You. I cherish Your presence and thank You for continually reaching into my heart and letting me know that You are here with me—now and tomorrow too. You are my portion and my blessing.

IN JESUS' NAME. AMEN.

WHEN GOD SAYS NO

It's easy to love God when He answers a prayer the way we want Him to, especially when He answers above and beyond what we imagined. But He doesn't always answer the way we hope. Sometimes He says yes but with conditions we hadn't thought of or expected. Sometimes He says yes but not yet—we must wait for its fulfillment to come. Then there are times when the answer is no—and that answer is hard to bear, especially when He's supposed to be a good and loving God. *How do you equate His love with a no, especially when you hurt through and through?* The same way a child trusts in his or her parents. A child can't possibly comprehend all the facets of life or understand the bigger picture, so there is no other option than to trust.

When God says no, it is an opportunity to accept that He knows better than we do, even when it doesn't make sense. Those are times to release the grasp of our own understanding and rely on our trust in Him.

*Lord, I simply don't understand why
You won't change my circumstances when I
know that You can. What I ask of You
is perfectly reasonable and makes sense
to me, so I don't understand why my prayers
are met with a no. Help me to accept that
You know better than I do and that every
answer to my prayers is for my good
and for Your glory. I love You and trust You
to be with me for another day as I walk
in Your grace.*

IN JESUS' NAME. AMEN.

HOLDING ON TO FAITH

The LORD said to Abram: Go from your land, your relatives,
and your father's house to the land that I will show you.
So Abram went, as the LORD had told him.

GENESIS 12:1, 4

Sometimes our faith in God is the size of a mountain, high and wide and immovable. Other times, our faith can literally shrivel to the size of a mustard seed. We can look to the faith of others who have gone before us, such as Abraham, who was called to leave everything he'd spent a lifetime building to "go" as God commanded. And there was Job, who suffered great loss in a very short time. But they both trusted God's plans over their own, even though they didn't know exactly how those plans would unfold.

Sometimes we are called to walk away from fruition as evidence of our faith. Other times, God allows what we have to be taken away. Both are testing grounds that stretch us beyond what we ever thought possible. We need Him as much in one situation as the other. Walking with God is not easy or predictable, but in the end, He is over all that we face, and He never stops working in us toward the purpose He's got planned.

Lord, it's hard to understand why You've allowed circumstances to obliterate my dreams and the direction I thought You were leading me to go. I need You to pick up the pieces of my life and steady my feet on solid ground. I want to say I trust You completely, but You know my heart and that I'm struggling. Please help to bring me to the level of trust in You that I need for living a testimony that points people to You and the good Father that You are. I hold on to You now and embrace the love I know You have for me.

IN JESUS' NAME. AMEN.

HIS FAITHFUL LOVE

The one who trusts in the Lord
will have faithful love surrounding him.

PSALM 32:10

There isn't anything much more comforting than knowing you are surrounded by people who love you and care. Their presence feels like a blanket pulled from the dryer and wrapped around your cold body—feeling the warmth soak into your very bones leaves you speechless. All you can do is stop, close your eyes, and sigh with thanksgiving for the relief it brings. It is the same with the presence of the Lord as He surrounds you with His Spirit of love, as well as those He brings into your life who reach out with concern.

While everyone has a wound to nurture at some point or another, God knows exactly where yours is and what it consists of. And in His compassion and grace, He promises to surround you in just the ways you need with His love, which never fails. There is nowhere the soothing warmth of His Spirit won't go in order to let you know, without a doubt, that He is right with you, and that He loves you beyond measure.

Father, I am so blessed to know that You surround me, just the way I am, and that I can truly rest in You. I take great comfort in knowing You are with me every moment of the day. Help me remember that You are the one, true Source of love and strength and hope in my life. I lean into Your arms and look to You for everything I need in order to do what You've given me to do today. I love You and trust You and feel so reassured by Your presence—there is nothing or no one like You. You satisfy my soul. You are Yahweh.

IN YOUR SWEET NAME, I PRAY. AMEN.

HE WILL RESTORE

The Lord says, "I will give you back what you lost
to the swarming locusts, the hopping locusts,
the stripping locusts, and the cutting locusts."

JOEL 2:25 NLT

When conditions are right, locusts (or grasshoppers) will band together and fly in swarms that completely decimate all vegetation in their path. The loss can be quick and vast, and unless witnessed with your own eyes, the destruction is almost inconceivable. One might think that the loss is so immense, it is beyond repair, but then again, our God is so immense, nothing is beyond His reach or ability.

So how have the locusts swarmed through your life? Have years been eaten by long-term illness? Have your dreams been eaten by financial crises? Have beats of your heart been eaten by rejection? Has your will to live been swallowed up by the loss of a loved one? The Lord says, "I will give you back what you lost." In His perfect time and in His perfect way, He is all about keeping His promises, including this one.

Lord, the hole in my heart is great, and my belief in restoration and repair is but a thread. I don't feel inspired to believe this promise, yet I will choose this day to embrace it as Your personal word to me. I hold on to what I know to be true about You and that is that Your Word is truth, that You love me, and that You are with me now. Thank You, Lord, for Your grace and mercy that fills my being as I walk with You through another day.

AMEN.

HIS GOODNESS
IN ALL THINGS

You intended to harm me,
but God intended it all for good.
GENESIS 50:20 NLT

Can you sing a hallelujah in your sorrow? Can there be praise in a heartbreaking situation? It's possible if we're convinced there is something praiseworthy to shout about. And when we remember the times past when Satan meant something for our harm, yet God turned it into something for His good, we can praise and thank Him for what He will do in our circumstances today—even when we can't see it. He may permit tragedy, but He doesn't let it have the last word.

It is in the darkness of the soul where songs worthy of our singing will spring forth because God is always up to something good—always. Nothing is wasted or beyond His ability and desire to form what we see as nothing but wrong into something that is altogether right. Where the limits of our sight end, the omniscience of His view begins, and He never stops working to bring His goodness one step closer to our hearts and to His glory. All praise be to Him.

*Father, I'm thankful that no matter what
I am facing, I know that You are good.
If I can't see anything to praise You for,
I can always praise You for what You will
do on my behalf. I cling to the trust I've had
in You in times past and the trust I hold on
to for my blessed and abounding future.
I believe You when You say that You intend
the details in my life to work together
for my good. You were in control yesterday,
and You are in control today.*

ALL PRAISE BE TO YOU. AMEN.

HOPE SURRENDERED, HOPE FULFILLED

You are God my Savior,
and my hope is in You all day long.

PSALM 25:5 NIV

When we or someone we know receives the diagnosis no one wants to hear, it's natural to hope for a miracle of healing and the sparing of pain or discomfort. Or when someone we love abandons us to stand in our grief alone, it's natural to hope for reconciliation and the healing of hearts that seem irreparable. Our prayers become supernatural channels of hope to direct our emotions, thoughts, and actions in a way that encourages us to believe that what we long for will happen.

But in those times, we know we aren't really in control of the outcomes, and we are challenged to surrender our hope to the One who has the final say. When we do, our hope surrendered becomes hope fulfilled in God, not in the outcome we hope for. When we truly surrender, His peace can then take hold and lead us through whatever we face each day with all glory pointing to Him.

*Father, I know I am not in control
of the circumstances I face, but I believe
that You are. I humbly look to You and
surrender my hopes and the outcomes
I long for. I accept that Your will should be
done, whatever that may look like.
I'm holding on to You now, and I need
Your peace to surround me and stay
with me as I walk through this journey.
I could not live without You leading
and guiding my way.*

WITH THANKSGIVING AND PRAISE,
I PRAY. AMEN.

PITCH YOUR TENT

From there [Abram] moved on to the hill country
east of Bethel and pitched his tent, with Bethel
on the west and Ai on the east. He built an altar
to the Lord there, and he called on the name of the Lord.

GENESIS 12:8

Abram was seventy-five years old when God uprooted his very comfortable and prosperous life. He instructed Abram, "Go out from your land, your relatives, and your father's house to the land that I will show you." His only map was the voice of God giving direction as needed, one day at a time. How did Abram hear God's voice? He pitched a tent—an altar—between Ai (a symbol of the world) and Bethel (a symbol of God) and "called on the name of the Lord."

Abram didn't know where he was going, but he wasn't lost. He had a Divine compass. When we pitch our tent—between what used to be and an unknown future—and we call on His name, God will answer, lead, and direct. The dependence Abram had is the same dependence we have on God today, and when we humbly seek His will, He is faithful to reveal it.

Father God, I bow down to You now
at the altar between what used to be
and the unknown future I am facing.
I need Your guidance, I need Your provision,
I need Your hand to help and to hold me
today and in the days ahead. I confess
I am lost without You, but with You,
every step I take is in Your sovereign power.
Take me where You want me to go,
and help me to do what You want me
to do. I trust You with today as well
as all my tomorrows.

IN YOUR HOLY NAME, I PRAY.
AMEN.

REMEMBER HIS MIRACLES

Depend on the Lord and His strength;
always go to Him for help.
Remember the miracles He has done;
remember His wonders and His decisions.

PSALM 105:4-5 NCV

Sometimes there are days, especially when grieving, when the comfort we seek from feeling at peace just can't be attained. It's when our spirit feels misaligned with God's. It's in these times when the best thing to do is stop, bring to mind the miracles He has done, and take time to ponder their significance.

We can look to the heavens—the stars, the planets, the galaxies—and the artistic brush of God's creation. And when we acknowledge this and take time to appreciate the scope of His hand, we walk in the presence of His love and can rest in assurance that if He orders and sustains the universe, He is all-sufficient for holding up our lives and nourishing our hearts for yet another day. This is why we can and should depend on Him for our strength and go to Him for help.

Father God, Your creation and the miracles
You have done, not only in the heavens
but in my life, bring me pause. Your beauty
and wonder are all that I seek today because
they are beyond description. They alone
bring comfort to me now and remind me
that You are in control and that You
are good. I'm grateful for the faithfulness
of Your love and the gift of Your creation
for me to enjoy. I lift all praise
and glory to You.

ALL GLORY BE TO YOU. AMEN.

HOLY BEGINNINGS

Who can separate us from the love of Christ?
Can affliction or distress or persecution or famine
or nakedness or danger or sword?

ROMANS 8:35

Troubles and sufferings, danger, even violent death are all circumstances where we certainly don't feel the presence of God's love. If anything, they are places where we feel abandoned and alone. But does that mean He isn't with us? Does it mean that forces of darkness have claimed victory over our lives?

Our enemy would have us to believe this. He's the voice that cleverly deceives us into thinking our pain is a valley of wasteland, where time, hope, and dreams will never be recovered. We are tricked into believing that, while we are stricken, life will pass us by without blinking or even caring.

But our valleys are not a means to an end—they are holy beginnings where the fullness of God will carry us into the richest fellowship with Him as never before. They are the intimate depths where God says, "I know you hurt and you don't understand, but this is where you and I will meet and abide as never before."

Father, I need You and want to abide
in Your presence as never before. I don't
understand the whys of all that I face,
but I trust You enough to believe that
this time is not wasted; it is not an end.
It's a redirection into a new beginning
of the life You have planned for me—
a life of love and abundance of favor.
I pray that the ways You will use me
and my circumstances will bring us closer
and fulfill the plans You've laid for my life.

ALL GLORY TO YOU. AMEN.

JOY IN THE BROKENNESS

*I speak these things in the world so that
they may have My joy completed in them.*

JOHN 17:13

Can there be joy in the core of a broken heart? The thought seems to contradict our natural way of thinking, but when placed in the supernatural realm of our Lord, He says there can be. That's because, when facing the darkest hour of His life, Jesus made clear that we are His joy—that means *you* are His joy. And His love for you is so great, His joy wouldn't be complete until He knew you could have His as your own. Nothing can stop His infusion of joy from pressing through to your heart, no matter what is happening around you. And when you let His joy in, you can become one with the one true Source of life.

So, if you are in the desperate state of having lost your joy, you don't need to work to find it. Simply claim the joy that is yours through Christ. He is ready to give it in abundance, because He loves you.

Lord, sometimes Your love is beyond comprehension. To know You are with me and that You care for me the way You do is a blessing and a relief. Because of this, you'd think my heart wouldn't be so heavy, yet it is. I sincerely need help with experiencing joy. Will you please give me Yours? Please lift my heart as only You can and help me to rest in Your presence. I want to go through this day glorifying You above and beyond whatever I face, and I know I can, as long as I have Your joy.

ALL GLORY AND HONOR TO YOU.
AMEN.

TAKE YOUR TIME

There is an occasion for everything,
and a time for every activity under heaven: . . .
a time to weep and a time to laugh;
a time to mourn and a time to dance.

ECCLESIASTES 3:1, 4

Time is one of the most important measures used for getting from one point to another, whether on a road trip or going through life. And the rule of thumb in this day is, the faster you get somewhere, the better. In some cases, this may be true, but on the path of grief, there is no timetable to meet. When traveling a journey of restoration, time may even stand still, and that's as it should be.

Just as the depths of wounds vary in size and destruction, everyone has their own pace for picking up the broken pieces of their heart and mending them back together. There simply isn't room for one to compare the amount of time he or she needs with someone else's.

God gives time in perfect portion in relation to what He knows we need. May we take one day at a time and rest in how fast or how slow He leads.

*Lord, thank You for the gift of time.
Please guard my heart and my mind
from comparing how much time I need
for healing with someone else's. Help me
to rest in each day that You give me
to process and repair my life. I want
to be whole again, and You know best
how to get me to that point. I love You
and trust in Your lead.*

IN JESUS' NAME, I PRAY. AMEN.

WHY, LORD?

*I am able to do all things through Him
who strengthens me.*

PHILIPPIANS 4:13

When anything bad happens, oftentimes the first question that comes to mind is "Why?" Sometimes, in God's grace, He reveals the answer, which we may or may not like, but there is at least some solace from the understanding we gain. What's really hard, though, is when He doesn't provide an answer and our thoughts are left to burn immeasurable energy trying to figure the answer out on our own. Then, sometimes, a tragedy is so immense, we don't want any answer—there isn't one that would be remotely acceptable.

But there is a catch-22 in asking why: When we demand to know the reasons behind what God allows, we are not abiding in a place of trust, and He wants us to trust Him with abandon. Jesus didn't feel like dying on a cross, but He trusted His Father so completely, He was able to endure and receive the strength He needed to fulfill God's plan. And as we trust in Him with full measure, we can have that same courage through Him who gives us the strength.

Father, I confess I want to know why You have allowed the circumstances in my life, both in the past and now. I want to make sense of what seems senseless and wrong. Help me to stop asking why and focus my mind and the condition of my heart when it comes to trusting You. I want to trust You in all things, not just some of them. Help me to remember and trust that You are for me, You are good, and You are in control.

AMEN.

FORGIVING OTHERS

Forgive us our debts,
as we also have forgiven our debtors.

MATTHEW 6:12

One common denominator we can find in many difficult circumstances is that of another person's actions that either caused or helped to cause the situation we are left to deal with. Someone else's misguided actions—or maybe even intentional ones—can affect a myriad of people's lives, including yours. It could be a drunk driver who killed a loved one, or someone who stole your life savings for drugs.

It is very hard to turn down the heat of anger and prevent resentment from growing without bringing in another denominator, and that is forgiveness. Without it, hearts harden, and lives never get back to a state of true peace, let alone experience any amount of genuine joy.

Forgiveness isn't a pass to let someone else off the hook. It's the key for saving our own hearts by placing them back into the mercy and love of a God who understands and promises justice in His perfect time and way.

Lord, it's hard to forgive. It's hard to trust again. It's hard to release my anger and my pain without seeking my own restitution. Help me to wrap my emotions around Your Word to forgive, even if I don't feel like it. It's the right thing to do and what it will take to move forward and find Your peace again. Please mend my heart and help usher my mind and spirit into a place where I can release my hurt completely to You, forgive my offenders, and trust You with the outcome.

TO YOU BE ALL THE GLORY. AMEN.

FORGIVE YOURSELF

Seeing their faith, Jesus said to the paralyzed man,
"My child, your sins are forgiven."

MARK 2:5 NLT

Another common denominator found in many difficult circumstances and hardships is something *we've* done to cause or contribute to the pain around us. We are not exempt from producing anguish—through our words, our actions, and sometimes even our inactions—and we ourselves must wade through it in the aftermath. And as important as it is to forgive others for the wrong and hurt they've brought on us, it is as vital to forgive ourselves for the times when we are the source.

Sometimes the hardest thing to do is allow the complete measure of healing that forgiveness brings into our burdened heart. Our memories are powerful—they will replay our actions over and over and continually highlight what we know we should have done differently. When this happens, there is, without a doubt, a reason to pause and remember that if the God of the universe is willing to forgive us, we must be willing to forgive ourselves as well.

*Father, I can't stop thinking about how
I would give anything to go back in time
and undo the wrong I've caused. I just
can't seem to get past my mistakes and
move on in true freedom. I ask for Your
forgiveness, and I need Your help forgiving
myself. Help me to hold on to the truth
that as I claim Your forgiveness, I am set
free from the bondage that unforgiveness
can cause. Thank You for loving me
to such depths that I cannot escape it.*

IN JESUS' NAME. AMEN.

HE HEARS, AND HE SEES

Can the one who shaped the ear not hear,
the one who formed the eye not see?

PSALM 94:9

What a comforting thought: God, who formed the intricacy of our ears and the complexity of our eyes, had a plan for their use—not just for us to communicate with one another, but to commune with Him. He sees us. He hears us. He is aware of every detail of need, whether physical, emotional, or spiritual. "Not a single sparrow can fall to the ground without your Father knowing it" (Matthew 10:29 NLT); therefore, we must know and believe that He sees and hears us all the more. After all, are we not worth more than even a flock of sparrows? (Matthew 10:31).

Our God has ears that hear; He has eyes that see—and it is our blessing to behold when we use our eyes to gaze at His face and our ears to listen for His voice of love, which He speaks so freely. Walk in this truth today and know that He is watching You now. You are not alone.

Father God, I look to You and find such assurance in knowing that You see what I'm going through, and You hear my cry right now. You are not a distant, uncaring God—You are One who remains close. Your heart of love listens when I call out to You, and Your eyes of compassion look at my need for mercy and _____. Help me to walk in this truth today and know that You haven't gone anywhere—You are right by my side and will never leave.

IN JESUS' NAME, I TRUST. AMEN.

HE LEADS AND PROVIDES

He brought water out of the flint rock for you.
He fed you in the wilderness with manna.

DEUTERONOMY 8:15-16

When looking at the story of God leading the Israelites out of Egypt, His miraculous provision is seen in numerous ways. First, He brought them a leader by choosing Moses to be the communicator between God and the people. God provided water out of a rock to quench their thirst. He poured down manna every day to fill their stomachs and give them strength. He also didn't let their clothes wear out, and with all the miles of walking over forty years, He didn't even let their feet swell. God covered all their needs throughout the entire journey from bondage into freedom.

Instead of Moses, we have Jesus to do our communicating—He is but a prayer and a cry away. His Spirit quenches our thirst for comfort and rest. His friendship fills our hunger for companionship, and His love is a guard to wrap around our hearts.

Wherever you are on your trek, remember He is present with you, leading and providing all the way.

Lord Jesus, thank You for being my closest friend. I need You to help me today. I ask You to fill the voids in my life with the presence of Your Spirit. Redeem the loss I've endured with restoration and new purpose. Give me the comfort and healing I need in all the places I hurt. Fill my heart of mourning with a deposit of Your joy. Renew my hope and help me to endure this road until my feet are firmly planted on new ground. Thank You, Jesus, for hearing my prayer.

IN YOUR SWEET NAME, I PRAY. AMEN.

PASS THE COMFORT

When others are troubled, needing our sympathy and encouragement, we can pass on to them this same help and comfort God has given us.

II CORINTHIANS 1:3-4 TLB

It's natural and common to want to withdraw when depression and hardship are our closest friends. But after a while, isolation can lead us—even draw us—into self-absorption, which is never good. When we do, focusing on our problems takes us off the heart of the Savior, as well as off the needs of others. It may sound like a stretch to muster up the effort to think of others, but if we have any spark of desire to turn our situation for good, it can be done by looking outside ourselves and being a comfort to someone else who is hurting. It's what Jesus did on a daily basis.

An ounce of compassion extended to another bruised heart can literally change the course of someone's life, including yours when you see and help someone else in need.

Lord, help me to look outside myself today
and see someone who needs an ounce
of Your love—then give it to them
through me. You bring comfort to me;
now give me the strength and insight
to bring comfort and encouragement
to someone else. I'm so grateful for Your
care and love for all who are hurting.

IN YOUR NAME, I PRAY. AMEN.

FROM OUR GOD
TO YOUR GOD

My tears have been my food day and night,
while all day long people say to me,
"Where is your God?"

PSALM 42:3

Our life is a testimony in the good times and the bad. When we succeed, people watch for how we'll handle the victory. When we work through a trial, people watch our response to the stress. And when we are knocked down, eyes are on us to see if God is really working in our lives. Is He as personal and intimate as we say He is? Will our actions parallel the words we speak about our faith?

It's a turning point where you may ask the same question for yourself because it's literally the place your heart may find nothing worth living for except the answer: He is Yahweh, and He is with me.. He changes from being *our* God to *your* God; from *our* help to *your* help, and from a friend we have in Jesus to a friend *you* have in Jesus. His hand of mercy and heart of compassion are not only ours; they are yours.

Father, thank You for being my God. Thank You for being my Savior and my friend. Thank You for knowing the number of hairs on my head and the places of my heart that are broken and hurting. I call on Your Spirit to surround me with Your presence. Hem me in and hold me close. Be my God in this moment and through this night. Even though tears have been my food day and night, may others see how close and personal You are. Let them see the lifeline You are—not just to me, but for them as well. My hope is in You, and I will praise Your holy name, my Savior and friend.

GLORY TO YOU ALWAYS. AMEN.

A CROWN OF LIFE

Blessed is the one who endures trials, because when he has stood the test he will receive the crown of life that God has promised to those who love him.

JAMES 1:12

Enduring a loss, continuing day after day in a state of grief, is probably the most difficult thing any of us will ever face. One thing that helps is to remember that to endure something means you're passing through. There is another side to come out of and step back into daily living that isn't necessarily absent of pain, but it's become secondary to the newfound joy and life that surrounds your heart.

James doesn't promise that the test of endurance fully ends before we reach our heavenly home, but he does promise that when we do cross into eternity with the Father, a crown awaits. It's a crown of righteousness that is free of pain, sickness, and tears, and it will be something to celebrate and look forward to with those who have gone before us. In the meantime, God's Spirit of love and comfort upholds even the weakest of hearts while He whispers and woos us unto Himself and keeps us going yet another day.

Father, I take so much comfort in knowing You are with me as I endure this season of pain. I don't know how long I'll be here, but just knowing I am not alone and that Your Spirit surrounds me is enough to sustain me through another day. I love You and keep looking forward to someday walking into renewed strength, a restored life, and a revived calling for whatever You have in store for me. In the meantime, I rest in You and the hope I receive from the love You pour onto me. I love You, Jesus.

IT'S IN YOUR NAME, I PRAY. AMEN.

HE WILL SATISFY

The LORD will always lead you,
satisfy you in a parched land,
and strengthen your bones.
You will be like a watered garden
and like a spring whose water never runs dry.

ISAIAH 58:11

None of us would knowingly or willingly journey through a desert for any length of time without a plan. Yet, there are seasons in life when circumstances can change so quickly, we don't have time to prepare for the events that unfold around us. We can go from life as usual to a wilderness journey, where we are lost without a compass for direction. God knew we'd have times of wildnerness, and while He doesn't say He'll prevent those times from occurring, He does promise to be with us and provide the sustenance we need.

He will "satisfy" us, which means that even though we may not have the daily comfort we once had, we will have the nourishment our body and soul need for repairing a heart that's depleted, broken, or crushed. His love reaches in and fills us with His very Spirit, which never runs dry.

*Father, You are the Giver of life. You are
the Sustainer of dry, parched souls
who call on Your name. I need Your
presence today to nourish my spirit
and bring renewal to my bones.
Turn my life into a well-watered garden
where new buds emerge and the fruit
of Your love brings a new harvest
in due time. I love You and thank You
for hearing my plea.*

IN JESUS' NAME. AMEN.

HE NEVER CHANGES

Whatever is good and perfect is a gift coming down to us from God our Father, who created all the lights in the heavens. He never changes or casts a shifting shadow.

JAMES 1:17 NLT

One perplexing thing about grief is that there are no switches to turn your feelings on or off. One minute you can be down, the next you can be somewhat normal, but then out of the blue, you might actually bear a grin with an ounce of joy only to be in tears a few minutes later. One small step toward healing can mean two big steps backward into the hurt, and it's hard not knowing what step will happen when. This is when you just want to hold on to something that remains stable for having balance.

In this ever-changing range of emotions, it's a tremendous comfort to know we have an unchanging God. He is the same today as He was since the beginning of time, and He'll be the same tomorrow and the day after. He's consistent, secure, dependable, and strong—just what's needed for keeping the soles of our feet and the depths of our hearts firmly planted no matter what currents we're in. He will not be moved.

*Father, I cling to You now and ask that
You keep me from getting swept away
by the currents of my emotions.
When I lack the strength and the will
to control the waves that carry me from
healing back to heartache, I ask that
You hold on and not let me go. Be my
anchor of security and steadiness
that nothing can or will change
as I draw from Your strength.*

ALL PRAISE TO YOU. AMEN.

SEEK HIS KINGDOM

Give your entire attention to what God is doing right now, and don't get worked up about what may or may not happen tomorrow. God will help you deal with whatever hard things come up when the time comes.

MATTHEW 6:34 THE MESSAGE

If a loved one has passed, your home is destroyed, your bank account is empty, or you're dealing with a long-term illness, it's difficult not to get swept up in fear—it can be paralyzing. Questions can quickly outnumber the solutions needed for figuring out what life will look like. Where will provision come from, especially when the bills and pressures surpass the resources for covering all the needs?

This is certainly nothing new; it has been the same since the beginning of time, which is why Jesus included these words of assurance we all need for keeping fear at bay and our faith front and center. He said to keep seeking, which means proactively looking for God's presence and the personal truths found in His Word. As we do—as we keep our eyes and thoughts in a posture of seeking Him—*we will find Him,* and we will reap the blessings of His miracles down to the finest detail.

Lord, help me to maintain my focus
on You and only You. Put a guard
around the eyes of my heart so that
all I can see is You. Your ways
are greater, Your solutions are better,
and Your plan is not an accident.
Give me more faith to truly believe
that You will provide—whether emotional,
physical, or spiritual—in ways that
Your righteousness is revealed in me.

I LOVE YOU AND WORSHIP YOU,
ALMIGHTY GOD. AMEN.

LOVE TESTED

God proves his own love for us in that
while we were still sinners, Christ died for us.

ROMANS 5:8

Love . . . From our human standpoint, we too often place conditions on our love for one another, as well as for God. This is because it's easy to love when life is going well, problems are few, and joy comes easy. But when a trial invades and lingers with no end in sight, will our love for God remain? These are the times our love for Him is tested: Can we, will we, remain in love with He who is the Giver and Taker of life?

Before answering, it's only right to remember that He didn't wait until our lives were in order before saving us. He proved His love by making the ultimate sacrifice of His Son before we even uttered a word about our love for Him. Shall we then hold fast in love even when we don't like the way life looks? While keeping our eyes on the lasting hope of eternity, let our answer be yes.

Father, it's hard to maintain a posture
of love when I want to give up.
Yet You haven't given up on me—I know
You're still with me as my ever-present help.
I choose this day to love You, even though
I don't understand what You're doing.
I choose this day to trust and believe
that Your love for me is as strong as ever,
and that, if nothing else, I can rest in that.

IN THE PRESENCE OF YOUR LOVE,
I PRAY. AMEN.

FROM IRON TO GOLD

As iron sharpens iron, so a friend sharpens a friend.

PROVERBS 27:17 NLT

Iron sharpening iron immediately brings to mind the thought of an iron blade being sharpened on another piece of iron. It takes material that's as equally strong for one to benefit the other. But what about the sharpening of our faith, our endurance, and the fortitude we need for enduring trials? If someone's a true friend, he or she will speak with honesty and challenge us not to take an easy road, but the best and highest road through difficult times. But where do we find such a friend?

Jesus says, "You are My friends if you do what I command you" (John 15:14). He is not only our Savior; He is the Friend who knows us better than we know ourselves. He doesn't leave us to be overtaken by our sorrows and cares—He uses them to build our faith and a spiritual life that cannot be overtaken by anything—including the trial you are facing now. See Jesus as your Friend and take hold of His hand. Trust that He is doing a good work in you that you may not see now but will discover over time.

*Lord, help me to see You in my situation
in ways that will make me a stronger
person. Use the difficulty I'm going through
to build my character and test my faith
in Your goodness. Help my belief in Your
presence, Your power, and Your purpose
for my life. Make the iron crown
I'm wearing now into a golden crown
that gives You all the glory.*

IN YOUR GREAT NAME, I PRAY. AMEN.

ONE DAY AT A TIME

"Live one day at a time."
MATTHEW 6:34 TLB

Live one day at a time . . . This sounds simple and easy to do, yet it isn't because our lives are not simple and easy. They are filled with complex details that can confuse, burden, complicate, and discourage a heart that's already holding on by a thread. Sometimes we have to utilize the "power of the pen" by literally writing or journaling what we are facing, then highlighting what can be done today, and letting the rest go for tomorrow.

If today includes being still, then be still. If it means accomplishing one task, then only do that task. If today is filled with the challenge to be grateful for one thing, then find that one thing and thank God with all your heart. The important thing to remember is not to allow unnecessary anxiety to creep in and rob you of this present moment, which is where God dwells. Right here, right now, He provides strength and hope for this moment in this day, one day at a time.

*Lord, help me to stop and be
in this moment—in this state of prayer—
with my whole heart. Guard my thoughts
and expectations of what I think should
happen today so that I can immerse myself
in the sweet spot of Your presence. I know
You never give me more than I can handle,
so please help me not to give myself
more than You say I should. Thank You
for meeting with me here and now
with the promise that You will be
with me tomorrow as it comes.*

IN JESUS' NAME. AMEN.

HIS RESURRECTION, YOUR STORY

Mary stood outside the tomb, crying.
As she was crying, she stooped to look into the tomb.

JOHN 20:11

Jesus was dead and buried in a tomb, and after three days, Mary Magdalene stood where the door of the tomb was cracked. She stood in grief beyond measure at the death of her Savior and peered inside with the hope of seeing His dead body. She thought His life was over, but we all know that the resurrection of His body meant His life was far from over. His story was entering a new beginning and purpose, and Mary was filled with joy and excitement she didn't see coming.

Likewise, friend, your story is far from over. Keep praying and watching for His touch, and when death and doubt are all that you can see, God, in His resurrecting power, will respond to your seeking heart the way He did to Mary's. His purpose in your life will never die. In the same way He created light from darkness in the beginning of time, He will bring new light and life into your circumstances.

Father, open the eyes of my heart
so that I can see and feel the power
of Your hand at work, writing a new story
for my life. Resurrect my will to live with a
seeking heart for whatever You orchestrate.
Please use what's happened in my past
to shape my future in ways that can
and will be used as a testimony of Your
faithfulness and love. Help me not to resist
where You lead, but rather walk with You
in complete trust as You redeem my loss
for Your greater good. Thank You for the
power of Your resurrection in me and the
hope it gives for my life.

IN JESUS' NAME. AMEN.

FRIENDS, OLD AND NEW: PART 1

I am dying from grief. . . .
my friends are afraid to come near me.
When they see me on the street,
they run the other way. I am ignored . . .
as if I were a broken pot.

PSALM 31:10-12 NLT

When the landscape of life changes during loss, we quickly discover that friendships we once thought would last a lifetime can dissipate. This isn't always true, but all too often it is. If you find yourself in bankruptcy, friends can be quick to judge. If you find yourself in a long-term caregiving role, friends can be few because of their own discomfort with death. In the case of divorce, friends end up choosing sides. Friends come and go, but that doesn't ease the sense of betrayal or abandonment we can feel.

One consolation, other than the fact that Jesus is a Friend who will never leave, is that there will be new friends to come who share a similar path of pain. People need people—we need friends—and God *will* work to bring in those who need you as much as you need them.

*Father, help me to walk through the changes
I face with grace. Help me to trust You
with the people You bring into my life,
both now and in the days ahead.
You know my needs, not only for comfort
but also for someone who understands
where I am and what I'm going through.
And thank You for being the closest Friend
I could possibly have.*

I LOVE YOU, LORD. AMEN.

FRIENDS, OLD AND NEW: PART 2

*Jonathan became one in spirit with David,
and he loved him as himself.*

I SAMUEL 18:1 NIV

N ot all friendships are meant to be lifelong; some are meant for a season. This happens when specific needs arise in your life and God so beautifully brings a new friend who blesses, enriches, and fills those needs in ways that can be surreal at the time. These are kindred spirits, relationships that are instinctive and natural and can form quickly.

But what also can happen is, as you begin to heal and move out of your pain, they don't necessarily move with you. The valley of grief is their purpose, but yours takes you to new pastures. What's important is to embrace the change with gratitude and not give in to feelings of guilt or obligation for what will be. God is constantly working so that our greatest need is for Him to strengthen and sustain us however He chooses. He is the ultimate Friend, who will usher us through the valleys our path takes us.

Father, I am grateful for the help and companionship of those You've brought into my life for such a time as this. I am also grateful for steps of healing and glimpses of my future that are bringing light and new purpose into my heart. Help me to be gracious and accepting of however You lead and whomever You choose to bring in and out of my path. I also pray for how You might use me to help someone else who's going through what I've been through—when the time is right.

ALL BLESSINGS AND GLORY TO YOU.
AMEN.

WHO DOES HE SAY THAT I AM?

*Once you had no identity as a people;
now you are God's people.*

I PETER 2:10 NLT

One thing a season of loss can bring is a loss of identity. One day you're married, the next you're a widow or single; one day you're a parent, the next you're childless; one day you're a top executive, the next you're unemployed. The identities we live under in our day-to-day experience can disappear in an instant, which adds a whole dynamic of adjustment to wade through. When someone says, "Tell me about yourself," or when you are filling out a profile, it's normal to hesitate and literally have to rethink who you are. This is the very reason to remember that, in Christ, you are His child, and that will never change.

When we are part of the family of God, the only "labels" we wear are those of *chosen*, *sanctified*, *redeemed*, and *whole*. Above and foremost, each of us is a member of God's family, whom He created and cares for. Any other label can change, but in Him, we are secure within our place of inheritance. That will never change.

Father, I'm sorry for the times I've allowed my identity to be rooted in what I've done or whom I'm with other than You. Help me to completely embrace the high status of being Your child, even if I don't "do" anything other than love and serve You. Help me to release who I thought I was and hold on to who I am in You and the security and comfort that brings.

ALL PRAISE TO YOU, JESUS. AMEN.

A SONG IN THE DARK

*About midnight Paul and Silas were praying
and singing hymns to God, and the prisoners
were listening to them.*

ACTS 16:25

There they were . . . After being beaten, imprisoned, and chained in a dark, cold, stench-filled cell, Paul and Silas prayed and sang hymns to God. One would think that yelling and cursing would be their response, yet they knew from their knowledge of and experience with Christ that, in order to rise above their situation, inspiring their souls was more vital than feeding their flesh—and praying and singing does just that. Singing praise to the Father is a direct line to the soul for building inspiration and refueling hope. Our singing through the night not only pleases the Father, but it allows others who are hurting—like the other prisoners—to see Christ and want to sing in their situations as well.

So, sing. From the depths of your heart, sing of your love and give praise to the One who hears and blesses not just you, but those around you.

Lord, I want to lift a melody to You today. Help me find a song in my heart to sing just for You, to show my love and adoration for all that You are. Fill my soul with more of Your Spirit and less of my pain. Help my song inspire others to sing so that they may be blessed too. I want to lift a sacrifice of praise to You because You are Yahweh and You are good.

IN YOUR GLORY AND SPLENDOR,
I PRAY. AMEN.

GOD'S PEACE
WILL OVERCOME

In everything, through prayer and petition with thanksgiving, present your requests to God. And the peace of God, which surpasses all understanding, will guard your hearts and minds in Christ Jesus.

PHILIPPIANS 4:6-7

It can happen in a flash and catch you completely off-guard: memories triggered by an everyday occurrence. You could be going to the hospital for a routine visit, only to realize it's where your loved one was last alive. You could be watching an old movie when the lines remind you of a friend who's now gone. Or what about a song playing on the radio that transports you to when you sang along with a child who once rode in your car?

These kinds of memories are ones we can either resist or accept. They're a reminder of the fine line we walk when grieving. There's often no telling when these memories won't hurt quite so bad, yet, over time, with thanksgiving, wounds do heal. When we give thanks for what time we *did* have with someone God molds our todays into a new purpose and calling in Him. A grateful heart allows His peace to overcome our sorrows from yesterday.

Father, I thank You for the love,
the enjoyment, the fulfillment,
and the experiences, for all the memories
from yesterday to dwell in my heart
and bless me today. I wish I had more time
to make more memories, yet I am grateful
for the time I had. I ask that You remove
my sorrow and replace it with Your joy.
I will carry it with me into my future
with a bright and hope-filled view.
My memories are mine—no one else
has them—and I'm so glad You have
given them to me. Thank You for mending
and healing my wounds, transforming them
into places I can freely linger
with a smile in my heart.

ALL GLORY TO YOU. AMEN.

HE FILLS OUR HEARTS

---

*For we know how dearly God loves us, because He has
given us the Holy Spirit to fill our hearts with His love.*

ROMANS 5:5 NLT

At the Art Institute of Chicago, there is a display
by a Japanese artist named Mineo Mizuno of an
oval, stone-like sculpture titled *Water Drop*. Mizuno
has created many *Water Drop* pieces, but the one
displayed at the Institute is different from the others:
There is a hole in the middle of the stone. He not
only left a hole, but he also left rough edges where his
fingers pressed to make the hole, and it is said he did
this as a way of expressing the void he felt from his
father's death. It's a very striking visual of what grief
looks like to so many of us who have suffered a loss.

Gazing at the hole—seeing a hole in anyone's
life—can leave feelings of emptiness and hopelessness.
Yet when we take into account the instilling of the
Holy Spirit in our lives, no hole remains empty. His
presence, His love, His healing, His compassion—they
fill to the brim and seal our hearts so that all we see
is a hole become whole. He is faithful to complete us,
all because He loves us so.

Father, I ask that Your Holy Spirit
fill me now in the cracks and brokenness
I know are in my heart. Fill the void
and emptiness I feel with Your presence,
Your joy, Your healing, and Your comfort.
May Your grace be all-sufficient for what
I need to move forward and experience
Your fullness. There is none like You—
no other solace or consolation that
soothes my soul and settles my being.
I'm grateful that You know my need
and You want to fill it.

YOU ARE YAHWEH, AND YOU
ARE GOOD. AMEN.

PAUL'S POWER, OUR POWER

God has not given us a spirit of fear,
but one of power, love, and sound judgment.

II TIMOTHY 1:7

When the circumstances of life change and the realization comes that what was "normal" will never be again, all the unknowns can produce a wall of fear we aren't sure how to climb. God understood this when He led the apostle Paul to write this verse from his prison cell. Paul could have given in to his fear and not taken the time or effort to write such encouragement to his adopted son, Timothy. Yet Paul claimed God's power as his own and ministered to Timothy's struggles that came with serving the church in Ephesus. Suffering from persecution, Paul challenged Timothy to remember that fear doesn't come from God and that he had the power to dispel his fear by claiming and holding on to the power he carried within his heart through the Holy Spirit.

We have that same power today—to keep forging ahead, to keep love alive, and to be of sound mind while doing the work God calls each of us to do.

Father, search me and know my anxious
heart. Show me where I've allowed fear
to reside and then deliver me from its
stronghold. I want Your Spirit of power
to rule within my heart above all else.
I want Your love for me to give me strength
to love and live in spite of how heavy
my heart may be. Please clear my mind
so it's free to think clearly for today and
for my future with wisdom and sound
judgment. Help me to remember that fear
is not of You, and that, with Your help,
I am able to dispel the clutches of its
influence at the sound of Your name: Jesus.

IN YOUR POWER AND LOVE, I PRAY.
AMEN.

ACCEPT ONLY THE GOOD?

[Job's] wife said to him, "Are you still holding on to your integrity? Curse God and die!" "You speak as a foolish woman speaks," he told her. "Should we accept only good from God and not adversity?" Throughout all this Job did not sin in what he said.

JOB 2:9-10

Of all the saints who've inspired millions through adversity, Job is one of the most tried and true. He spent his life serving and honoring God, only to lose almost everything he'd worked for, as well as suffer physical illness beyond comprehension. Yet he "did not sin in what he said." His wife's response was to curse God and die, which seems harsh, yet how many of us can relate? It seems only natural to blame God for allowing tragedy to destroy what we've worked for or dreamed of for so long.

Yet in his wisdom, Job maintained and acknowledged this simple truth in God's sovereign order of things: "He . . . sends rain on the righteous and the unrighteous" (Matthew 5:45). Job's testimony of love was to accept the bad as well as the good. It's not an easy kind of love, but it's one we are all challenged to possess for the Giver and Taker of all things.

Father, I confess I'm angry at times for what You've allowed. I don't understand why, after all my efforts to serve You, You've permitted adversity to wipe away my dreams and what I hold dear to my heart. Right now, my hurt outweighs my heart, and I need Your help with accepting that You allow the bad as well as the good. I pray a covering of Your grace as I work through any attitudes that are not pleasing to You, and I pray this in all humility, in light of Your patience and compassion.

IN YOUR NAME, JESUS. AMEN.

TRIALS . . .
FOR OUR GOOD?

We are pressed on every side by troubles,
but not crushed and broken. We are perplexed
because we don't know why things happen as they do,
but we don't give up and quit.

II CORINTHIANS 4:8 TLB

For grapes to become wine, they must go through the squeeze of a winepress. For caterpillars to transform into butterflies, they must force their way through the narrow channel of a chrysalis. And for our faith to grow and mature, we must pass through trials that at the time seem unbearable, yet we do not get crushed. The apostle Paul would know—he faced more trials than most, and he didn't give up and quit.

Our trials are the only portals that lead to true transformation from our dependence on ourselves into an absolute reliance on our almighty God. We need them in order to fully comprehend just how out of control we are and how fully in control He is. And if we will cling to the fact that there's an eternal perspective in play, we will persevere and reach the most beautiful heights only the saints who endure are able to see.

Lord, please help me to rise above my immediate circumstances and strive for the eternal perspective You want me to have. Give me the determination not to give up— on myself or on You. Help me remember that while I may have trouble on every side, as long as I stay by Your side, I can and will endure. I trust that You will hold me up and keep me going for yet another day.

IN YOUR GREAT NAME, I PRAY.
AMEN.

PRAISE HIM IN ALL THINGS

*Through the praise of children and infants
you have established a stronghold against your enemies,
to silence the foe and the avenger.*

PSALM 8:2 NIV

When our hearts are tender and feeling downcast, it's normal, even healthy, to simply feel what it needs to ride the emotional waves that wash over us. Healing doesn't come without the feeling that leads up to it. But there are also times on the road to recovery when praise is the very best balm for getting through the most difficult places of all. The heartfelt cries of love and adoration from the "children and infants"—or rather, the most vulnerable among us—quench the enemy's hold on sadness and overcome it with joy and grace. Praise is the tune that drowns out the voice of darkness and leads the way toward our Father's presence of peace.

Praise in the midst of pain leads the way, parts the waters, depletes the enemy, and silences our hearts so that all we hear are the words, "I love you, dear one. I am with you. I will help you. And I will never leave."

Father, I praise You now. Even though I am buried in grief, I praise You for Your help, Your presence, the hope You give, and the purpose You bring. You are good. You are love. You are mercy. You are grace. You are what I need for coming out on the other side of my circumstances feeling restored and whole, and blessed in ways I never thought possible. Establish in me a stronghold of love for and dependence on You as never before. You are my life and my reason for living. I lift all my praise and glory to You.

AMEN.

GOD OF ISRAEL, GOD OF YOUR LIFE

He led [Israel] through the depths as through a desert.
He saved them from the power of the adversary;
He redeemed them from the power of the enemy.

PSALM 106:9-10 (EMPHASIS ADDED)

The Israelites were held captive for years, and God made a way for their freedom. But He didn't just make a way—by parting the Red Sea—he was their personal escort. As much as they wanted freedom, He knew the conditions of their hearts were worn and the level of their faith had been tried. They not only needed Him to make a way, but they needed guidance, protection, and continual hope to keep moving forward.

Therefore, God *led* them into the miraculous. But He didn't stop there, He *saved* them against all odds from the enemy. He *redeemed* them from the consequences of all the sin—both their own and their enemy's. And as you work through days, months, maybe even years of captive pain and hardship, He will lead, save, and redeem you and your circumstances for your good and His glory. The same God of Israel is the same God of your life.

Father, give me pure and simple faith
to believe Your promise to lead, save, and
redeem my life. Part the waters and torrents
of difficulty and put my feet on dry land
to step forward into my future with hope
and joy. Help raise my voice to sing praise
to You for what You have done and for
what You will do to make my crooked way
straight and to heal my heart. You are
my Helper, and You are faithful to complete
in me what You started from the time
I was created.

ALL GLORY TO YOU. AMEN.

FINDING THE MEANING

*We were buried with Him by baptism into death,
in order that, just as Christ was raised from the dead
by the glory of the Father, so we too may walk
in newness of life.*

ROMANS 6:4

We have an innate need for purpose and meaning in life. We ask, "Why am I here? How does my infinitesimally small existence matter?" Finding answers to these questions hits especially hard when we are in a pool of grief and all we can do is try to stay afloat. "Where is the meaning in my miscarriage? in my divorce? in the loss of my legs or my sight?" This leads us to ask, "Is there significant meaning in death, no matter its form?"

Death may not have an obvious headline about its purpose, but there is always an option to look for it in the core of loss. Just as we sort through rubble after a fire, there can be found a seed of life that, when nurtured and fed by the natural forces of hope-filled sorrow, a new sprout will emerge, a new blade of life we would never have known otherwise will grow. It is in Christ's death that we discover a new birth and a new purpose for eternity's sake.

Father, I don't understand how there can be any good purpose in the loss I am facing, but I trust You. Please don't let my circumstances be all for naught. Please be working Your goodness so that someday, in Your time, I will see new life and find new meaning that brings solace to my heart. I want there to be a day when I can look back and see how Your hand has worked the details of my broken heart in ways that only You can.

IN YOUR NAME, I REST AND TRUST.
AMEN.

GOODBYE TO GUILT

You have seen my affliction.
You know the troubles of my soul
and have not handed me over to the enemy.
You have set my feet in a spacious place.

PSALM 31:7-8

Recovering from trauma of any kind doesn't come with a "one path fits all" approach to healing. But there is one element that can work its way into many sufferers' journeys no matter how personal it is, and that is guilt.

There is the guilt of surviving an accident when your friend didn't. Guilt that you can go on living after your spouse has passed. Guilt over a mistake you made that caused someone else's harm. Guilt from finally feeling happy again after mourning for months or even years. There's just no way around guilt, and while working through it, it's easy to want to backstep and self-destruct.

Yet God says, "No! I am Yahweh, and your guilt is not of Me. I have the power and the authority to take the guilt that you carry. In exchange, I give you My love—to propel you forward into a spacious place to truly live again."

Father, sometimes it's hard to feel good and right about my ability to live when a loved one has gone. And sometimes I struggle to let joy and happiness come into my life— guilt won't allow it back into my heart. I need Your help to feel comfortable with healing and moving on without the weight guilt brings. Please take it now; release me from its stronghold. Help me to receive Your power and Your love so that I can recover over time in healthy and life-giving ways. You have the ability to restore, so now give me the courage and the blessing to receive it.

IN JESUS' NAME, I PRAY. AMEN.

HE IS OUR PEACE

*"Peace I leave with you. My peace I give to you.
I do not give to you as the world gives.
Don't let your heart be troubled or fearful."*

JOHN 14:27

These words from Jesus are so comforting and true. He's made it so that, no matter how low our posture, we can breathe in His peace, which brings comfort to the deepest degree of pain we are in. It scatters every ounce of fear that the enemy has instilled. It calms the most violent of cries from a broken heart. His peace brings supernatural order to chaos and stillness in the soul that surpasses all human ability or logic. His Spirit of peace resides in us in full measure when we relinquish our own efforts and will into His hands and keep Him in the forefront of our hearts. His peace isn't what the world says will help us, but the world doesn't know Him.

Jesus came not only to proclaim peace for all the nations, but for our hurting hearts as well. Let us all abide in it today and the next. It is good for all time.

*Lord Jesus, I need Your peace. I breathe it in
now and ask that You guard my heart from
anything that tries to take it away. Your
peace is life to my soul. It sustains
my every step and thought and move that
I make as I pick up the pieces of my life.
You are the Giver and Sustainer of all that
I need. I rest in that today and bask
in the serenity I can have no matter
the mess that's around me. I love You
and rest in Your love for me.*

IN YOUR GREAT AND MIGHTY NAME,
I PRAY. AMEN.

WHAT DO YOU WANT?

Jesus stopped, called [the two blind men], and said,
"What do you want Me to do for you?"

MATTHEW 20:32

As Jesus traveled from place to place, it was not unusual for Him to ask those He encountered what they wanted (see Mark 10:36, 51). And as He encounters you in your state of sorrow, He wants to know the same. What do you want? He is listening and waiting, but sometimes sorrow can bury the answer so deep down that we don't think to pull it up and ask.

Do you want Him to ease Your pain? Do you want Him to tell you what you're supposed to do now? Do you want Him to perform a miracle? Do you want His help with making sense of your life going forward?

We know that Jesus doesn't always give us what we want, but He clearly wants us to ask, because what He wants is dialogue. He wants us to talk to Him about our deepest needs. He wants us to approach Him and speak honestly from the heart without holding back. He wants to help, and the first place to start is answering His question: "What do you want Me to do for you?"

Lord Jesus, I want _____.
I want Your peace and comfort right now.
I want Your help navigating through
my pain while keeping up with the daily
business that living on this earth requires.
I want Your help with making sense of
things and the direction You are taking
my life. I want Your help with healing
and restoration. I want Your Spirit to fill
the emptiness that is in my heart. I want
You to show Yourself to me today. I want
to see You in the details that surround me.
I want to know You are with me.
I want You.

IN YOUR HOLY NAME, I PRAY.
AMEN.

GOD-ALIGNED
EXPECTATIONS

---

*He will keep in perfect peace all those who trust in Him,
whose thoughts turn often to the Lord!*

ISAIAH 26:3 TLB

We all have dreams of what we think we want our life to look like in the present as well as in the future. But when the reality of what we've dreamed of is nothing like what we had hoped and planned for, pain, anxiety, and worry can and will creep in and steal our peace. Disillusionment, even thoughts of failure and loss of hope, can leave a person numb and frozen, wondering what direction they're supposed to take next.

When this happens, the only way to get the perfect peace Isaiah proclaims is when our thoughts turn from our disappointment to a renewed trust in the Lord. This means gathering old expectations and relinquishing them to God, where His sovereignty is our foundation and where a clean slate for new beginnings awaits. It's having both palms open to God's plan instead of our own and truly trusting that His is better.

Father, I confess the heartbreak I feel
because of unrealized dreams. It's so hard
to pick up the pieces of brokenness
and move on. I want and need Your peace
in my heart and mind so that healing can
do its work in the depths of my soul.
Yet, so often, it feels out of reach.
Help me to release my will and what I
used to dream for. Help me to start over
with a renewed focus on You and a
willingness to trust that Your way is always
the best way. I need Your healing,
I need Your guidance, and I need
Your embrace that assures my heart
when I abide in complete trust in You.

ALL GLORY TO YOU. AMEN.

HE IS THE LIVING GOD

When [King Darius] reached the den, he cried out in anguish to Daniel. "Daniel, servant of the living God,". . . "has your God, whom you continually serve, been able to rescue you from the lions?"

DANIEL 6:20

King Darius wasn't a follower of almighty God—Darius considered *himself* a god—yet that didn't stop the influence Daniel's belief in the one, true God made on him. Not only did the king see that Daniel's God was personal and real; he saw that Daniel's God was *living*. He wasn't an idol or a mortal human such as himself—Daniel's God had active power to bless and sustain even in the direst circumstances. So, after Daniel spent the night in the lions' den, the king acknowledged the power God had for saving Daniel's life.

That very living God from Old Testament times is still living today. And whether your faith has waned or remains steadfast, nothing will stop Him from actively reaching into your own lions' den to help you as you need. God was and is to come, in your life now and in the days ahead, to rescue you, comfort you, protect you, and restore you into the new life only He can give.

Father, I believe—help my unbelief.
Help me to remember that You haven't
gone anywhere—You are alive and working
now, as You have been since the beginning
of time. I may face death all around me,
but You are living and breathing into my
circumstances as I pray to You this very
moment. Through everything, I look to You
for new life and new hope and new reasons
for living for You and being a light that
influences others the way Daniel did.

IN YOUR GREAT NAME AND POWER,
I PRAY. AMEN.

WHAT, ANGRY WITH GOD?

Then Jacob was left alone; and a Man wrestled with him until the breaking of day.

GENESIS 32:24 NKJV

There comes a point in the grieving process when anger sets in and grows. Anger at our situation, anger at the finality loss brings, anger at not being able to go back and change things, even anger at God. But the good news about being angry with God is that, first, in order to be angry with Him, you have to believe in Him—we normally don't direct anger at nothingness. And believing in God, believing He exists, is the first step toward true healing. The second reason is that He understands. Jacob wrestled all night with God, and God remained engaged. He got into the ring with Jacob until he was worn down—then God blessed him.

It's a magnificent thing to know we can be real about our feelings and emotions with the One who made them. And it's a beautiful thing that He allows us the time and space to direct it all toward Him—no matter how unpleasant it is. As a result, He gathers our messes and turns them into blessings we wouldn't have received otherwise, all in His time.

Lord, I confess I'm angry that You allowed
tragedy to occur in my life. I'm angry that
after all the years I've served You, this is
what I get. I'm angry that my dreams
have been shattered, my plans have come to
a stop, my service to You seems for nothing,
and my love for You doesn't feel returned.
And yet I know that You do love me.
I just don't understand why and how
You could cause or allow such difficulty.
Please, God, help me get back to loving
and trusting You as I know I should.
Please take my anger and replace it
with Your comfort and Your rest.

I ASK THIS IN JESUS' NAME. AMEN.

A LIVING DEATH

Love is patient.
I CORINTHIANS 13:4

We usually equate death with something that no longer physically lives. But another very real and deep grief sets in when someone we love still lives but physically leaves. We know they're out there, yet we cannot see or speak to them anymore. A wayward teenager may suddenly move out without a goodbye; a sibling may reject and ignore our attempts at contact; a lifelong friend may cut us off after a heated misunderstanding; a close relative may get lost in drug or alcohol addiction. It's literally a living death, and finding finality is difficult for bringing closure on this side of heaven. The grieving process can draw out indefinitely because the hope of reuniting is still there.

These are the circumstances when patience of heart is tested beyond unimaginable limits and brings home the words of the apostle Paul: "Love is patient." But patience of this magnitude hurts and can lead us to ask, "Just how much patience are You talking about, Lord?" To which God would say, "How deep is your love?"

Father, I continually draw from the faith I have in You to help me through the sadness of circumstances beyond my control. Lead me into a place of acceptance for what is and fill me with enough grace to keep my hope-light burning. It is my desire to remain close and true to You, trusting You in all things, especially when I don't have the answers or outcome I want. Thank You for being patient with me time and again. When I feel like running out of patience, give me more one day at a time. And whatever happens, whatever may be, I go back time and again and say that through this journey, You are enough.

IN YOUR GREAT NAME, I PRAY. AMEN.

THE ROAD OF FIRSTS

"Seek first the kingdom of God and His righteousness."
MATTHEW 6:33

After a loss of any kind, life changes direction onto a new road, and that is a road of firsts. There's the first day and night without a loved one by your side. There's a first decision made without their input. Or how about the first meal, even a first holiday where there's a vacant chair at your table. Every day is the first day of something into each new season to follow, which can be unsettling in and of itself. Firsts can be scary because the terrain is new and you're not sure where it will lead except to a new loneliness.

One thing we can do throughout that first year is meet each first with another first: "Seek first the kingdom of God." When we seek God first, when we look to Him first and release both what we do know, as well as what we don't know, into His hands, the terrain isn't a matter of uncharted territory. It's a matter of returning over and over again to the safety and comfort of the One who is over all and who is working on our behalf to bless our path of healing.

Father, I seek You today and give all that is to come to You. I look to You and trust You to provide the comfort I need, to instill the peace Your presence brings, and to fill the void I have in my heart with Your Spirit so I'll know I'm not alone. Be my companion each step of my way this season, this year—however long I need for adjusting to my new life with You. Thank You for Your unending love and mercy all my days.

IN YOUR NAME, I PRAY. AMEN.

YOUR FUTURE, GOD'S PLAN

"I know the plans I have for you" . . .
*"plans for your well-being, not for disaster,
to give you a future and a hope."*

JEREMIAH 29:11

Hanging mobiles are so perfectly balanced that if one of the items that's attached is suddenly cut off, the entire mobile tilts off-center. This is very much what you can feel like when you've lost a spouse or a loved one. Nothing is the same. Old routines become disjointed; questions about how to pay bills or maintain the car become overwhelming. What will the future be now that the dreams you've had for years will no longer happen? If not for our loving and caring God, it's a mindset that could lead downward into despair.

But while the future we envisioned no longer exists, the future God has planned for us does. The difficult places we find ourselves in are already interwoven in ways that create a whole new landscape for us to walk into.

Father, right now, the horizon of my future looks blank—I have no idea what it's going to look like anymore. I hold on to Your promise that You have plans for me, and that they are good. You know the desires of my heart even better than I do, and I trust You with them now, to bring them together in ways I can't see. I cling to You as You pick up my broken pieces and seal them back together with a new design You know will be a blessing in the end.

THANK YOU, JESUS. AMEN.

SEEING EACH DAY
AS A GIFT

Teach us to number our days carefully
so that we may develop wisdom in our hearts.

PSALM 90:12

There is some gain that is found in loss, and it is sincerely appreciating the time we have with loved ones still with us. The lessons developed from being more in the moment, seeing others with more intention, and not taking for granted the simple joys and beauty around us become more the rule than the exception. As the psalmist writes, "Teach us to number our days carefully," there is the reminder to be more deliberate about how we live, where to focus our attention, whom we spend our time with, and slowing down enough to absorb the moments we are given throughout each day. There is wisdom in this alone, not to mention the blessing of feeling more fully alive. Each day is a gift from God, and this often becomes more apparent when recovering from bereavement. It's one of the hidden joys that lie in the depths of sorrow—to truly live one day at a time and rejoice in His surrounding goodness.

*Father, help me to grasp the joy that is mine
when I surrender to being in each moment
with all my attention. Let me not miss
the gift of family and loved ones who are
with me. Rein in my thoughts to be here
in the present, not in the past or the future.
Help me to simply be "here" right now
and see the gift of Your touch in my life
and in others'. Teach me to slow down
and be wise about spending time in places
and doing what You'd have me to do,
however You lead. Don't let me miss
the small joys You place on my path
of healing and restoration. Help me to see
each day, each moment, as a gift from You.*

IN YOUR NAME, I PRAY. AMEN.

GET UP, PICK UP, AND GO

[Jesus] told the paralytic— "I tell you: get up,
take your mat, and go home." Immediately he got up,
took the mat, and went out in front of everyone.
As a result, they were all astounded and gave glory
to God, saying, "We have never seen anything like this!"

MARK 2:10-12

What a miracle. This man had suffered paralysis since birth and was judged by the scribes as being a sinner. He was the lowest of lows in society, yet Jesus walked into the picture and healed him on a Sunday, of all days—not something that was acceptable by the laws the scribes and Pharisees lived by.

Jesus is many things, and Healer is at the top of the list—He healed everywhere He went. He wants us to have victory over sickness and death, even when all odds are against us. And He wants the world to know about Him through our testimonies of His goodness. This is a clear and strong message to us today: Our lives, our tragedies, our healing, our stories that display the touch of His hand—they are what He's about. We are meant to rise. We are meant to get up, pick up our mat, and go.

Lord, I am ready. I want to get up. I want to pick up my mat. I want to go again. And I know that through Your healing presence in my life, I can do all of that. Be with me, help me to rise today, even if it's just one step up from the ground I've been lying on. Strengthen my heart to get up and pick up my mat so I don't return. Lead me into a new place to be where healing can soak in and where I can get back to the new path You have for me. Make my life a story that points others to You and the goodness You have shown to me.

ALL PRAISE AND GLORY TO YOU.
AMEN.

MOMENTS OF MENDING

Water will gush in the wilderness,
and streams in the desert;
the parched ground will become a pool,
and the thirsty land, springs.

ISAIAH 35:6-7

When living with a heart and soul filled with pain, we can become so burdened that we lose the will to see good. Our focus is fixed and frozen on the state of our circumstances. But God understands these times and causes the parched ground on which we stand to become a pool of refreshment. This can come through the song of a bird, a flower pushing up from the ground, the coo of a baby, the wag of a dog's tail. To mend a broken heart and spirit takes time, but only when it is laced with moments of reprieve that catch and hold a new gaze, a new joy, be it ever so small.

It's okay to break away from grief. It's needed for rebuilding and refreshing the soul. Make time to look for God's blessings and cling to the refreshment they bring. God, in His compassion and grace, wouldn't have it any other way.

*Lord, help me to see You today. Help me
to take a break from my grief and look
for Your goodness that is all around.
Fill my heart with small sparks of joy
that help to hold up my head and keep me
in a true state of hope and healing.
Help me not to feel guilty for wanting
to break away from the brokenness
I feel and be surrounded by the refreshing
moments You want to pour over me.
I love You and thank You for giving me
the desire and courage to move beyond
my despair and into a new optimism,
even if only one moment at a time.*

LORD, BLESS ME AND KEEP ME
IN YOUR HANDS THIS DAY. AMEN.

DEAD BONES RISING

"Dry bones, hear the word of the Lord! This is what the Lord God says to these bones: I will cause breath to enter you, and you will live. . . . Then you will know that I am the Lord."

EZEKIEL 37:4-6

Seasons, journeys, and valley experiences are all passageways for processing grief to whatever degree or time we need, but it is good to remember that they are periods we are delivered through, not places to remain. As God's breath continually enters our lungs, His healing power is instilled, and the dry, dead bones within our soul do come back to life. It won't be the life we once knew—it will be new terrain where balance is regained, and fresh purpose is brought forth out of the changes from the past. Our reason for waking up each day transforms from a spark to a flame that propels us forward in our thinking, our actions, our work, and our joy. And while memories may remain, they are framed with a new lens of love that only God can give. Then we will know that He, indeed, is the Lord and our broken hallelujahs have not been in vain. All praise be to Him.

Father, thank You for healing. Thank You for bringing me forward one day at a time in Your perfect and gentle way so that I can begin to live again. I need You more than ever to walk with me as I adjust to the changes and newness around me. Help me to see the touches of Your love and embrace them as the special gifts they are. Help me not to be afraid of life looking different than it used to. Help me to make wise decisions about my future as well as enjoy what You have in store. Thank You for being with me through my valley journey and for the countless ways You've blessed and comforted me beyond measure.

IN YOUR GOODNESS AND GRACE,
I PRAY. AMEN.

FLOWERS IN THE DESERT

The desert and the parched land will be glad;
the wilderness will rejoice and blossom.
Like the crocus, it will burst into bloom;
it will rejoice greatly and shout for joy.

ISAIAH 35:1–2 NIV

It's both encouraging and inspiring to know that even desert land contains seeds of life underneath all the colorless landscape we see with the naked eye. That is the greatness of our God, who, in His time, produces sprouts of new growth, new color, and new hope from a dormant heart. The crocus flower is small and low to the ground, but it's mighty enough to push forth through the final layers of a winter snow, producing signs of life we would otherwise not even know existed—but it does. It may be life of a different hue and form, but life it is, waiting to be noticed and received simply for what it is.

While our lives—our stories—may take us into the depths, His resurrecting power will bring us back into a new joy if only we will see it and embrace it as our own. His joy is what makes us complete and able to begin again, one day at a time, and it's ours for the taking.

Father, thank You for the seeds of life and joy You have planted in my heart. Help them to grow and find their way into view so I can follow Your lead out of the depths and into new pastures where I can move forward. I am grateful for Your timing and Your gentle ways of painting new landscapes filled with color for me to enjoy. Help me to see that each new sign of life You put into my day is of You and it's okay for me to walk in it.

IN YOUR HEAVENLY GRACE, I PRAY.
AMEN.

JOY IN THE MORNING

Weeping may stay overnight,
but there is joy in the morning.

PSALM 30:5

Over time, there comes a point when the landscape of deep, dark mourning will evolve into a lighted meadow with streams of new life calling out your name. *Having* to get up each day changes into *wanting* to get up and learning what a new "normal" life will look like. It's a very personal point of realization that no one else can know but you. It's also a point at which others will offer their own opinions, whether asked for or not.

"Don't you think it's time to get out and start living again?" Or how about "Don't you think it's a little fast for you to be going out and doing all that you're doing?" The voices can create confusion in your mind and leave you feeling vulnerable to judgment no matter which way you turn.

One thing is for certain: God promises us joy in the morning—He doesn't intend for us to stay overnight indefinitely. Your morning may be next month, or it may be next year; just be sure to embrace it when you and you alone are ready and with no second-guessing.

Father, thank You for the promise of healing and newfound joy that only comes from You. Thank You for the knowing that at some point, I will be able to accept more that life will be different, but only when I'm ready. Help me to put aside the comments of others and hear only You and Your voice of assurance that it's okay for me to move forward as You lead. I want to be in the center of Your will, not someone else's. I trust in You and thank You for the healing that You bring.

IN JESUS' NAME. AMEN.

TIME TO GO

The Lord said to Samuel, "How long will you mourn for Saul, since I have rejected him as king over Israel? Fill your horn with oil and be on your way."

I SAMUEL 16:1 NIV

After Samuel informed Saul that he would not be king, God, in His graciousness, gave Samuel time to mourn. After all, it was a very difficult task to bear the bad news after a years-long relationship with Saul, then never to see him again (see I Samuel 15:34–35). But after a time, God got to the point where He urged Samuel to get up and get back to living again. God had work for Samuel to do, and in God's sovereign wisdom, He knew it was time. Samuel was still grieving—the pain still lingered—but even so, God wanted him to get up again and get back to the new purpose He had in store.

This means that we, too, must get to a point where we are willing to fill ourselves with the power of His Spirit, get up, and once again, go. We may go in slow motion and lack our normal zeal, but the point is just to go and trust in God's perfect timing for what He has planned. He is constantly working in and through our trials, and He can do mighty things even when we're still down.

Father, thank You for time to heal and simply let myself feel what I need to feel. I know my life will never be the same, and I'm not sure what the future looks like anymore. But please help me at least to get up and start moving once again. Help me to receive Your strength for carrying out Your new purpose on my life, wherever it leads. I love You and trust in Your perfect timing.

IN JESUS' NAME. AMEN.

A NEW SONG

To all who mourn in Israel,
He will give a crown of beauty for ashes, ...
praise instead of despair.

ISAIAH 61:3 NLT

Some of the most beautiful pieces of music have been written from the wellspring of a broken heart. Horatio Spafford wrote "It Is Well with My Soul" after losing all four of his children on a sunken ship. Joseph Scriven lost his fiancé the day before they were to be married. After recovering from his loss, he fell in love again, only to lose his new fiancé just weeks before they were to be married. From that loss he wrote "What a Friend We Have in Jesus."

The list of songs written from tragedy is extensive—there are probably too many to count—and they are testament to the beauty that can rise from the darkness of a cavern. They are a miracle of grace to show that what our enemy purposes for our harm, God will turn into the healing splendor of His goodness. That was true centuries ago, and it is still true today.

Will you open your heart to a new song from God?

Lord, please don't let my pain be for naught. Help me to dwell in the depths enough to hear and learn a new melody of love over my life. Help me not forget that as dark as I feel inside, You are still working a new song within me that will be a testament of Your grace and of new wine pressing out. Create in me beauty for the ashes I see; give me a new heart of praise from my despair. I want this story, this season of my life, to count in ways beyond my imagination. I count it a privilege to lift my burdens to You in prayer today.

IN JESUS' GREAT NAME. AMEN.

THE PATH TOWARD VICTORIES

I will never leave you or abandon you.

HEBREWS 13:5

Going through a season of grief is not only about processing pain from loss and figuring out what life will look like going forward. It's also about healing and moving toward the victories that come from stepping out of a valley. There comes a point when we will look back with gratitude on how He's been there day after day to provide what we've needed. There can be a fear that God won't be as "there" as He was, because the need for His help doesn't feel so great. But the truth is, we need Him in the victories that await every bit as much as we need Him in the valleys.

Facing and stepping into new seasons that lead to a mountaintop bring their own challenges, especially the looming feelings of guilt for moving on. There's also the fear that God won't be as present because we think His primary focus is not those who are becoming strong, vital, and healthy. He will continue to be "there" day after day to counter false guilt with His truth and to reassure us that He will never leave. Ever.

Father, as I heal and begin to move forward into the new purpose You have for me, I hold on to You as tightly as ever. Guard me from false guilt for feeling joyous and full of life again. Continue to make Your presence known to me as new doors open and my heart beats strong again. I'm thankful You're a God of life and restoration that brings a newfound confidence and strength. I praise You and thank You for healing power and for a love that never fails.

ALL GLORY TO YOU. AMEN.

TIME TO REBUILD

After destruction or loss of any kind occurs, there comes a point when it's time to clean up the blocked pathways, sunken rooftops, and piles of rubble and begin to rebuild. Lifting one armful of debris can feel like moving a twig from the redwood forest, but progress can be made. Soon clear walkways, solid roof joists, and wide-open spaces behold the goodness of God. One by one, each fragment of sadness and sorrow are escorted out, and the joy that's been waiting is welcomed back into our sphere by a heart that's able to receive it.

When this happens, life doesn't look as it did before. There's a new depth to your foundation with and dependence on God, which is always good. He wants to appear in His glory in your set of circumstances, so you have no doubt that He loves you and is with you yesterday, today, and in all your tomorrows.

*Lord, thank You. Thank You
for hearing my prayers leading up
to this time in my journey. Thank You
for each step I'm able to take toward
healing and knowing that while things
won't be the same, all will still be well.
Thank You for all the glimmers of hope
You send for a new future, whatever it may
look like. Thank You for the new depth
of love I feel for You and for knowing
more than ever that You are with me.
Thank You for rebuilding my heart
into one that is whole again.*

JESUS, IN YOUR NAME, I PRAY.
AMEN.

YOUR STORY—A VESSEL

Jesus told the crowds all these things in parables,
and He did not tell them anything without a parable.

MATTHEW 13:34

There is power in story. That's why Jesus spoke in parables to the crowds, time and again. Everyone can relate to them as the mind quickly latches on to events that spur the imagination. Our lives are a story unique to us that no one else can declare. And while Jesus gave narratives long ago, He's unfolding them still through each circumstance we face. While we do, others are watching and listening, even cheering us on toward victory as we do the same for them.

So, what will your story tell? Will it lead back to the love of the Father? Will it reveal His miraculous hand on your heart? Will others want to follow your steps—even through difficulty and pain—so they can meet the Savior in ways they never knew? May the answers be yes, just as Jesus said when He accepted His fate on the cross. His entire life is about being led to the Father—and about us following. May ours do the same.

Lord, I want my life to matter for a bigger purpose than myself. I want what I'm facing to be nothing compared to the glory and honor that You deservedly receive. Hold my heart and guide my steps to close any gap of unbelief and doubt so that I am closer to You than ever before. Grow my faith and establish my feet to stand in Your honor and walk in Your ways so that others will want to follow and find You for themselves. Make my life story into a vessel that leads to You and the love You desire to give to all of humanity.

I PRAY THAT ALL GLORY POINTS
TO YOU. AMEN.

TOPICAL INDEX

Dear Friend,

This book was prayerfully crafted with you, the reader, in mind. Every word, every sentence, every page was thoughtfully written, designed, and packaged to encourage you—right where you are this very moment. At DaySpring, our vision is to see every person experience the life-changing message of God's love. So, as we worked through rough drafts, design changes, edits, and details, we prayed for you to deeply experience His unfailing love, indescribable peace, and pure joy. It is our sincere hope that through these Truth-filled pages your heart will be blessed, knowing that God cares about you—your desires and disappointments, your challenges and dreams.

He knows. He cares. He loves you unconditionally.

BLESSINGS!
THE DAYSPRING BOOK TEAM

Additional copies of this book and
other DaySpring titles can be purchased
at fine retailers everywhere.
Order online at <u>dayspring.com</u>
or
by phone at 1-877-751-4347